Soul Over Matter

Soul Over Matter

*Ancient and Modern Wisdom
and Practical Techniques to
Create Unlimited Abundance*

DR. AND MASTER
Zhi Gang Sha
Adam Markel

MARILYN TAM

WILLIAM GLADSTONE

BENBELLA BOOKS, INC.
DALLAS, TEXAS

BenBella Books, Inc.
PO Box 572028
Dallas, TX 75357-2028
www.benbellabooks.com
Send feedback to feedback@benbellabooks.com

Printed in the United States of America
10 9 8 7 6 5 4 3 2 1

Library of Congress Cataloging-in-Publication Data is available.
ISBN-13: 978-1-942952-58-9
e-ISBN: 978-1-942952-59-6

Copyediting by Stacia Seaman
Proofreading by Michael Fedison and Brittney Martinez
Indexing by Clive Pyne Book Indexing Services
Printed by Lake Book Manufacturing

Distributed by Perseus Distribution
www.perseusdistribution.com
To place orders through Perseus Distribution:
Tel: (800) 343-4499
Fax: (800) 351-5073
E-mail: orderentry@perseusbooks.com

Special discounts for bulk sales (minimum of 25 copies) are available.
Please contact Aida Herrera at aida@benbellabooks.com.

Contents

Part Three: Create Unlimited Abundance

Introduction
by Adam Markel

IN 2013 I was leading an event in La Jolla, California, when a good friend and respected business leader introduced me to a man named Dr. and Master Zhi Gang Sha. A medical doctor and a traditional Chinese medicine doctor as well as a grandmaster in tai chi, qi gong, *I Ching*, and feng shui, Master Sha is now renowned as a spiritual healer, lecturer, and eleven-time *New York Times* best-selling author of more than twenty books.

After our introduction, Master Sha surprised me by asking if he might offer a blessing to my students, and I found myself with a decision to make.

The group that day was no tiny breakout room with a dozen chairs. There were over three hundred attendees there for a three-day event. What's more, they were people who were experiencing their very first introduction to New Peaks, the company I led. As always, I was obsessed with ensuring that this first experience was one that delivered. We had delivered training programs to over a million people in over a hundred countries, and I knew it was that focus on delivering the highest value to our students that had helped us succeed.

I'm no skeptic. I may be a former attorney, but I'm very spiritual, and I lead much of my life and teaching from that perspective. Without a doubt, though, I am also *practical*. It was this practical side of me that immediately spoke up. Was introducing this mysterious soul healer I'd just met really the right way to begin a three-day immersion experience?

My heart told me, "Go for it." I knew that everyone who attends one of our sessions is there for a reason. And I also knew from experience, that reason at the deepest level is almost always a desire for *healing*.

Who better to kick off the day, then, than a healer of Master Sha's background?

But my head—my inner lawyer, you might say—told me, "Hang on. You don't even really *know* this guy." What if this blessing from a stranger made the wrong impression?

Thankfully, I went with my heart. Master Sha delivered a blessing that not only was magnificent on its own, but also created an intensely sacred space for us to work in for the next three days.

That moment of decision was the beginning of my friendship with Master Sha, and it's also a great example of a duality that is at the heart of this book and, indeed, our world. In trying to make my decision that morning, I was shifting between two states—my rational head and my intuitive heart.

This head/heart division is a duality we're all familiar with. We've all faced moments when, caught between two states, we can't seem to decide. It's a common experience, and when you begin to look around, you'll see this dichotomy everywhere. You'll discover that, like yin and yang, left and right brain, head and heart, visible and invisible, there are two sides to everything, as inseparable as north and south or right and left.

Nowhere is this duality more evident than in the world of money. Money is charged with head and heart conflict. Do we choose the job that pays better over the one we love? Do we save for the future or enjoy our money in the present? Is it wrong to pursue money? Are we penny-wise or pound-foolish? Money is a morass of conflicting emotions, polar opposites, and contradictions. Even our currency has two inseparable sides—the heads and tails of a coin.

Like metaphorical heads and tails, Master Sha and I began to talk on a regular basis. We exchanged teachings, and I learned more with each conversation about the world of spiritual healing in which he worked.

When I heard that he had a thirteen-part public television special coming out and was looking for a venue for a small preview party, I immediately offered my home. My wife and I hosted the event, a memorable evening that included Master Sha performing several special healings. It was also a great opportunity for more discussion between us.

During that party, Master Sha commented that New Peaks did much work to help people create more financial abundance. He, in turn, did healing work for people and companies, specifically by cleansing negative karma, helping many with challenging physical issues heal and recover. Like yin and yang, head and heart, we realized that our own duality might just hold the key to something special: The two of us, with our different but inseparable approaches of mind and spirit, could help guide people through the ever-challenging world of *money*.

As a business leader and former attorney, I would teach the "head" side of money—the tools, mind-sets, techniques, and thinking. Master Sha, the spiritual healer and teacher, would delve into the "soul" of money—the invisible realm of karma, spirit, and energy.

The result of that collaboration is this book—a unique way of creating abundance by learning to understand, attract, and manage your finances through the lenses of both the mind and the soul.

The Roots Create the Fruits

In our New Peaks programs, we focus on teaching people that the physical things that show up in their lives—everything from their homes to their health—begin as thoughts.

There's good reason for this. Thoughts lead to feelings, feelings lead to actions, and actions lead to results in life. It's what we call the process of manifestation, and it's why one of the first things we want to help people do is to pivot their thinking; to shift from negative to positive thinking, for example, or from less-empowered thinking to more-empowered thinking.

An easy way to think of this process is "the roots create the fruits"— what's below the ground, or invisible, creates what is above the ground, or visible. When an apple seed below the ground germinates and sends roots out, it creates an apple tree above the ground and eventually, apples.

This idea is one that we take for granted in nature when we see a tree grow, but to truly accept that this is a universal law, one that is at work not just in the woods and fields, but also in our own lives, is often challenging. We accept that apples in the present come from apple tree roots set down in the past, but we can find it surprisingly difficult to see how money (or lack of it) now might be related to roots set down in months or years prior.

The essence of this philosophy, and what matters most for your life, is the idea of *cause and effect*. Right now, the "fruits" you're receiving in life, from your income to your health to the quality of your relationships, exist because of seeds you planted in the past. Those seeds began as thoughts—things you were taught about money, for example, or beliefs you had about genetics and health—and eventually flourished into the fruits you see now in your life in the form of money, energy, and good health. *Your thoughts were the cause. What you have in your life now is the effect.*

From here, it's not hard to see where we need to go to change our results in life. If you want to see new financial fruits—greater income, a nicer home, more security—then you need to set new roots. You need to start thinking differently so that you feel differently, act differently, and eventually, *receive* differently.

What Master Sha brings to this equation is something much deeper. From his study of ancient wisdom and teaching, we know that the roots are deeper and *further back* than just your childhood or your thinking from a few months or years ago. It begins before your thoughts. It begins with your *soul*.

Yes, you can create dramatic results in your life by changing your thinking. You can, in effect, learn to understand and master the idea of "mind over matter."

But there's a deeper truth. Your soul is what controls the outcome. It's the original root of all the results. It's not mind over matter so much as *soul over matter*. Deeper roots bring sweeter fruits.

Your Money Roots

If you accept the cause-and-effect equation for your financial life, you might well wonder exactly how your financial roots were planted. If money—the fruit—is a scarce resource in your life today, where and when were the roots set?

While the money you spent on your credit card last month is an easy culprit to point to, your true money roots were planted much deeper and much longer ago. For most people, the seeds of their figurative "money tree" were first sowed in childhood, by their parents and early money experiences.

Like many of us, you likely have some very disempowering opinions and conclusions about money planted in that early, fertile soil. Read the following sentences and see if you can fill in the missing words:

> *"Money is the root of all _____."*
> *"Money doesn't grow on _____."*
> *"It takes money to _____."*
> *"The rich just get _____."*

Most of us can fill in these blanks with hardly a thought. They're expressions—seeds—that landed early in our soil and germinated almost immediately. They were then watered and nourished by our family, peers, teachers, and colleagues for years until they delivered the fruits we see today.

Like everything, however, these early seeds and their fruits have a front and back all their own. For all we've learned about the negative influence of money, we've also spent much of our time and energy in pursuit of it. We've been raised and taught to abhor and fear money, yet we devote much of our lives pursuing it. We've been trained to try to attract it and avoid it at the same time!

The result is that most of us have a confusing view of money. Whether you realize it consciously or not, there's a good chance the money seeds you planted early on in your life are conflicting with your current needs. You have mixed thoughts and emotions about money. On the one hand, money is important, helpful, and desirable. On the other hand, money is for the lucky few or for the extraordinary. You might believe money is for those who have done something wrong to receive it, or only for those who receive it as a family legacy. It's a confusing message, and the outcome is that although you desire abundance, your trees are bearing scarcity.

When we're young, the "soil" where we plant our first roots is very fertile. What we plant then tends to grow robustly, and the roots are stubborn. It's not impossible to change those roots, but they're well entrenched. The result is that when it comes to money, we've got one foot on the gas pedal and one on the brake. We're pursuing it and running away from it at the same time. We feel proud of our income and ashamed of it in the same instant.

And that leads us to financial trouble, every time.

Self-Sabotage: How Your Early Financial Roots Can Trip You Up

My dad was a civil servant. My mom worked a part-time job. While we weren't poor, money was never abundant, and I certainly never heard from my father that money was important. Instead, I heard things like "The rich get richer and the poor stay poor." He would speak, from time to time, about successful people as being greedy. About how it was hard to get ahead without already being wealthy or taking advantage of someone.

As a result, I grew up resenting wealthy people. In my mind, there was something unethical or immoral about wealth. But at the same time, I pursued money. After all, life seemed easier with money, and my family always seemed to have less of it than we needed. As a hardworking guy who made it to law school and into legal practice, I eventually got my wish and made a bunch of money early in my life.

So there I was. A young man programmed to feel that wealthy people were somehow *flawed*, but on the road to becoming one of those very people. What did I do? Naturally, my subconscious found some excellent ways to ensure that I got rid of that money. By lending it inappropriately and investing it poorly, I was easily able to ensure that I didn't become one of the "greedy rich."

This type of self-sabotage is exceedingly common. It happens below the level of our awareness and is a direct result of a disconnect between the roots we've planted and the fruits we seek. Until we change our money roots, we'll experience all the symptoms of a "root-fruit" disconnect, such as:

- an inability to attract more money
- poor or disastrous results in investments
- a near-constant sense of financial lack
- financial conflict with partners and loved ones

Anywhere you find conflict, stress, or anxiety about money, you'll find a disconnect between the roots of your past and your wishes for the future.

Planting New Roots: Financial Literacy

Not only are many of us not born *into* money, none of us were born to *do* money either—to understand it, attract it, nurture it, and spend it wisely. We're not taught how to manage money, and we're rarely even given a healthy view of it. If anything, what we're taught is counterproductive to financial abundance. We've been taught, in large part, by people who either didn't have any financial abundance or who had been taught their own negative, conflicted money message.

The current state of our financial literacy is one that plants seeds of scarcity. The good news is that we can change this. We can learn to see money differently. We can reinterpret the teachings and the experiences of our parents and grandparents.

When I started my process of creating new roots, I began with reading. I consumed books of all types but, in the financial arena, there were several that jarred my thinking so much that it was as if I could feel new roots spreading their first early tendrils into the soil of my mind.

Secrets of the Millionaire Mind by T. Harv Eker was one of the first books to reveal to me that changing my *thinking* would change my financial results. I didn't need to work harder, I needed to *change my mental programming.*

Rich Dad, Poor Dad by Robert Kiyosaki taught me how the poor, middle class, and rich *think* differently and how their finances reflect that different thinking.

The Millionaire Next Door by Thomas Stanley showed me how the wealthy upper middle class thought and, as a result, *acted* differently in managing their money.

These books were a revelation to me—I can't recommend them enough. Moreover, they point to what is likely a gaping hole in your own financial literacy. I found the whole process astonishing. Why was I discovering this information in my thirties and forties? Where was this knowledge when I was an impressionable child and a young man beginning my career and making critical choices about my future?

I realized that not only did I have no respect for money, I had no *understanding* of it. I didn't understand compound interest. I didn't grasp the great things money could bring to my life in the form of freedom, security, and charity.

Slowly but surely, I began to build my financial literacy. I read the *Wall Street Journal* and books by Peter Lynch. I began to change my thinking and, as a result, my feelings and actions.

Slowly, I began to create something in my life that I'd never experienced before: *financial harmony*. Where before I only had conflict, I now felt a growing sense of possibility and *peace*.

There's an expression: "Where attention goes, energy flows, and results show."

If you think something is unimportant, you don't give it attention.

What if, for example, you thought your children were unimportant? You wouldn't spend time with them. You wouldn't pay attention to them, try to nurture them, build their character, or teach them. The likely result of that lack of attention and energy would be a lack of "results" in your relationship with your kids. In other words, you wouldn't have one.

Financial literacy is a way of saying, "Money is important." It's a way of directing your attention to money so that you can give it time and energy and, in turn, receive results. It's the first step on the road to planting new roots and discovering the peace and abundance that can be created from financial harmony.

The Rich Person Inside You

Early on in my own efforts to plant new roots, I read a lot. One of the books that gave me an enormous "aha!" moment was Robert Kiyosaki's *Rich Dad, Poor Dad*. His astute insights into the differences between the rich, middle class, and poor, seen through the lens of his relationship with his father and his mentor, resonated deeply with me. I'd experienced the same conflict myself.

In more recent times, Robert's path and mine have crossed several times. He and I were having dinner one night in Melbourne when a simple moment of reflection highlighted the inner financial conflict that we all experience.

When the bill arrived at the end of the meal, Robert picked it up. As he scanned the bill, he looked up at me and said, "You know, it's interesting. I drive a Ferrari. I have plenty of money and property. But I still look at the bill. I still check it. Is it accurate? Does everything add up?"

"For all my money," he said, setting the bill down, "I still have a poor person that talks to me inside."

I immediately knew what Robert was talking about. I too had grown up with my own "poor dad," and I'd heard that inner "poor" voice many times. It was the voice that had helped me, I now realize, lose much of the money I'd earned as a lawyer. It was that voice that helped me spend my money unwisely and invest it thoughtlessly.

Robert, as you can no doubt guess, also has an inner rich person speaking to him, but his point is a powerful one. We *all* have a rich and a middle-class and a poor person inside us. There's nothing wrong with that. The real question is: *Who are you listening to?*

Robert drives a Ferrari. But, like you and me, he still has a poor person inside him. The difference is that he's aware of it, and he knows which voice to listen to, and when. He knows there's a time to check the bill carefully and a time to listen to the rich voice. He knows that both voices can contribute to financial literacy and abundance, *as long as you know who's speaking at any given time.*

The poor person inside you will never go away. Much like a fear that you've overcome, the feeling never goes away entirely, but what does happen is that you learn to recognize it when it comes along. You learn to say, *Ah, yes. Hello, poor person. Thanks anyway, but I'm going to ignore you right now. I know you might have something to offer in another situation, but right now I need to listen to someone else.*

Although you may not have been born with money or with the skill to manage it, *there is a rich person inside you.*

Your choice is whether to nurture that voice so that it speaks loud enough for you to hear.

List of Figures

PART ONE

Before Soul Over Matter

1

Mind Over Matter

A COMMON WITTICISM on the concept of mind over matter is *if you don't mind, it don't matter.* This is usually said in a deprecating manner, indicating that anyone who believes in the power of mind over matter is delusional or gullible. Of course, if you are facing a firing squad and your only defense is to use your mind to alter the direction of the bullets, mind-over-matter thinking is not going to help you.

In everyday life, however, the principle of mind over matter can be very effective and is not for the gullible or delusional at all. As with any universal principle or law, you must understand the dynamics of the principle in order to effectively achieve the results you seek.

The first recognized teacher of the principle of mind over matter in North America was a successful self-made business leader and entrepreneur from St. Louis, Missouri, named Charles Haanel. In 1912, he created a course called The Master Key System, which he sold as a mail-order course in twenty-six installments for ten cents an installment. The Master Key System was a major success. One of the early readers of the mail-order course was a journalist named Napoleon Hill. Napoleon Hill went on to write the most popular book ever published on the topic of generating and maintaining wealth, titled *Think and Grow Rich.* This book is still in print, with more than seventy million copies sold since publication. The Napoleon Hill Foundation is still going strong and releases multiple titles annually by individuals and organizations that espouse the effectiveness and importance of mind over matter in generating financial abundance.

As authors, we applaud the success and contributions of Haanel and Hill in bringing awareness of the importance of a proper mind-set and attitude to creating wealth, health, and happiness. In this book, we are expanding on the principles and techniques of mind power to add the even stronger soul power in causation and manifestation. In future chapters, we will explore *soul over matter* in depth, with specific examples on how soul generates mind reality. In this chapter, we want to help you understand the logic of mind over matter and demonstrate the correct interpretation of this basic yet powerful principle.

On the simplest level, mind is primary to matter because you cannot create any product or service until your mind has imagined it first. With the exception of the entertainment industry, the world of work and money is not in the practical sense a world of make-believe or wishful thinking. (Of course, money itself is a commonly agreed-upon fantasy about the value of certain pieces of paper and the concept of currency itself. We will discuss more about that in the next chapter on the history of money.)

A misunderstanding of the original work of Charles Haanel and Napoleon Hill has engendered the association of mind over matter with wishful thinking. In The Master Key System, Charles Haanel developed the principle of the universal mind, from which all mental images are derived. Haanel explained how, through meditation, it was possible for anyone to access the universal mind, and he gave concrete examples of how he did it himself. In The Master Key System, Haanel also developed the concept of the law of attraction. The original formulation of this law was that the positive energy you emanated drew positive energy to you, including good health, good relationships, and financial abundance. In the popularization of Haanel's work in movies and books such as *The Secret*, the impression was given that you merely had to visualize what you desired and you would attract that object to you. In terms of manifesting wealth, creative visualization is a helpful tool and technique, but not a primary causal process. It is true that if you are unable to imagine success or visualize a positive outcome in your business dealings, you are much less likely to manifest success. Creative visualization alone is equivalent to removing a blockage that might prevent success, but it is not an action that will actually create your success. As the late, great baseball player and homespun philosopher Yogi Berra stated, "I wouldn't have seen it if I hadn't believed it." Lack of belief can derail you, but belief alone is rarely sufficient.

Since you are reading a book that purports to provide modern and ancient practical techniques and wisdom to create unlimited abundance, you of course want to know what is needed to manifest. The full answer will be revealed in the following chapters that explain the role of the soul, but the initial answer is quite simple. Within your mind you have access to the tools, ideas, attitudes, and knowledge that have the potential to create unlimited abundance. This is not conjecture. This is fact. Millions of people with no more knowledge, education, social standing, or desire than you have become multimillionaires and enjoyed lives of material abundance. Each self-made millionaire/billionaire and those who inherited wealth and grew rather than squandered it followed his or her own unique path, but all of them used their minds and not their bodies as their primary resource for creating wealth. Stories of how people with imagination and visualization have transformed their existence to become much more joyous and abundant in many ways abound. One of the author's associates was born to a tenant farmer living in Caruaru in northeastern Brazil in the late 1940s. His parents were illiterate, and at the age of six he started working in the fields. He was able to learn basic math from other illiterate farmers whose lives focused on growing and selling vegetables, but he never went to school and never learned to read or write.

But this young man was extremely industrious. He worked hard and realized he could help the other tenant farmers by renting a wagon and taking their produce to market along with his own. This saved the other farmers' time and allowed them to spend more time in their fields cultivating and harvesting more crops. They were delighted to pay this young man a small commission on the sale of their produce. Word spread about the young man and soon he was focusing full-time on buying and selling the crops of all the tenant farmers in his district. Being observant, he noticed there was a boom in the prices for coffee, so he encouraged his farmer friends to plant more coffee. In a few years, he became the largest provider of coffee beans to one of France's premier coffee brands. When overexpansion and poor financial management

prevented the French company from paying their debt to their sup-
plier, this illiterate Brazilian became the owner of the coffee company.
Concerned that he might be overinvested in coffee, he looked around
and saw that beef prices were rising. Within five years, he became the
largest cattle rancher in the entire state of Pernambuco in northeastern
Brazil.

There are many similar rags-to-riches stories that have occurred all
over the world. Our goal is not to inspire you to abandon what you are
doing to seek a quick road to riches. Our young Brazilian friend worked
for more than twenty years before becoming a multimillionaire, and, in
his fifties, he did finally take the time to learn to read and write. Your
road may be long or short, and the role of your soul will determine the
length of your journey to riches. Our goal is to help you understand
that the path to financial abundance will always have thinking prior to
action. Whatever your present life circumstances, a proper mental attitude can potentially lead you to unlimited abundance.

One of the primary principles of both mind over matter and soul over
matter is that you must have a "why" in what you do that benefits others. The more you serve others, the more you are likely to receive. The
more you serve others unconditionally, the greater your likely reward.
The financial benefits may not come immediately, but they will come.
Although we may all question it at times, the universe is ultimately
fair. Good deeds and good thoughts are rewarded. The universe is also
infinitely abundant. There is no lack in the universe; there are enough
atoms and molecules, enough time and space, for every living creature
in the universe to enjoy the fullness of their being. Any scarcities you
perceive are man-made situations, the majority of which can be resolved
through man-made actions and inventions. To create these inventions,
it is quite helpful if you can access the universal mind. It will also be
necessary at the present time to understand the dynamics, history, and
role of money, which we will explain in the next chapter.

2

A Brief History of Money

N O ONE KNOWS for certain when money was first invented. We know that money is a man-made invention. No animals have ever created a system of barter or trade that involves money. Although there are instances of animals hoarding food, there is no evidence of animals trading foods or goods. Animals for the most part live in the present moment and are not primarily concerned about the future. Money is mostly about the future.

Money is a marvelous invention. It allows human beings to not just barter and trade but to create and plan. Physical goods and resources can be magically transformed into storable, durable, lightweight currency in its myriad forms: paper, checks, credit cards, electronic transfers, bitcoins, and so on. This magical ability to set aside resources for future needs without creating additional work was a breakthrough without which modern societies could not have evolved.

Of course, once money was created, human ingenuity took over and numerous ways of utilizing money were devised. Money experts emerged and, along with them, the concept of banks, and eventually our present economic systems evolved. Capitalism today favors those with large sums of money at their disposal. Money itself under capitalism generates money whether or not the owner of that money contributes to the production of goods and services. To some extent, this has always been true from the beginning of moneyed societies, but never to the extent of today's modern capitalism. In many ancient societies, it was considered immoral to charge interest when lending money. Money was considered a tool and a mechanism to benefit the entire community and to ensure trade and commerce, but not to create tiered societies in which some groups controlled a disproportionate percentage of the wealth of their community. One of the clearest demonstrations of a society that valued economic parity is documented in the indigenous potlatch ceremonies in the Pacific Northwest Coast of Canada and the United States, where every year the wealthiest village members would hold festivals during which they shared or even gave away the majority of their possessions, in effect trading material goods for social standing and prestige.

In the majority of primitive civilizations, people had few possessions and little ability to store possessions for future needs. Even today there are Amazonian tribes who move with the seasons, carrying all of their possessions with them and recreating living quarters from whatever plants and trees might be growing around them. These and other nomadic peoples barely recognized the concept of private property. When hunters caught a wild boar or other animals, everyone shared the meat. When the hunt was especially abundant, there would be festivals and celebrations, and neighboring tribes would even be invited to share their bounty. Oftentimes these invited guests would become allies and share their bounties, creating a safety net against less abundant times.

Individual tribe members had differing statuses, but these distinctions were based on inherent abilities and not on accumulated wealth. A skillful healer would be venerated as a shaman, and his or her knowledge of the medicinal value of plants would be highly valued and honored. A great hunter would have status, as would a wise leader who could guide community decisions, but their rewards were not more possessions or greater accumulated wealth.

As human beings moved from hunting to agriculture, the accumulation of property became possible. People developed fixed, permanent villages where they could build structures to store grain and other commodities. Once accumulation became possible, there was a true need for currency to enable economic trade and economic planning. A farmer could sell his excess wheat, buy a goat or cow to supplement his diet with milk, and diversify his dependence upon a single crop or activity. A goat herder could sell goats and invest in buying seeds to diversify as well. In the beginning, these simple transactions could be handled by bartering, but with the invention of money, the ability to involve multiple members in a transaction not only accelerated the frequency of such transactions, but created transactions that could have never occurred through bartering alone.

Scarcity Is a Human Invention

One of the unexpected outcomes from the evolution of money was the creation of scarcity. That's right. Before money, there was no scarcity. This does not mean that there were no instances of calamities, which resulted in starvation for an entire community, but there was no *relative scarcity*. There were no rich or poor; everyone had similar possessions and "economic" opportunities. There were those with greater status, those who had more wives, those who had more power, but in hunter-gatherer societies that did not use money, there were no significant economic differences. There was no scarcity as we think of scarcity today.

Scarcity is a concept that relates to having insufficient resources to accomplish a task or goal. For most wildlife, scarcity is related to natural cycles of the seasons, the migration of food sources, or the impact of seasonal change. Nature in and of itself has no scarcity. There may be drought and other weather-related challenges that create less abundance of resources, but generally there is a group survival instinct in the animal kingdom.

The relationship to scarcity for human beings is quite different. With the advent of money, opportunities were created to hoard money and to use money to control basic goods and services and to develop and control luxury goods and services. In the process, ever-increasing economic disparities have formed to such an extent that today the wealthiest one-tenth of one percent of humans on our planet own and control more resources than the poorest fifty percent. A consequence of this economic pattern is that over one billion people on planet Earth today live in abject poverty, barely able to generate enough money to feed themselves and their families.

This economic disparity and daily experience of scarcity by billions of human beings is not a natural development or an unavoidable consequence of a free capitalistic system. Of course, no one wants to be among the bottom billion and since you are reading this book, it is unlikely you are. In the following chapters, you will learn specific techniques that will ensure that your experience of scarcity will be limited or absent. Paradoxically, you will learn that part of your overcoming scarcity will include helping to reduce the scarcity of the less fortunate.

Prosperity Rituals

One of the most-used statements of scarcity in the world is "I can't afford it." If personal finance were a category on *Family Feud*, *I can't afford it* would be the number-one statement on the board.

For example:

- I'd love to go to Hawaii, but *I can't afford it.*
- I'd love to hire someone to help me with my business, but *I can't afford it.*
- I'd love to move to a nicer neighborhood, but *I can't afford it.*

They're all statements of scarcity. But if you dig deep, there are two critical things to understand about these kinds of statements:

First, scarcity statements are habitual.

We tend to think and speak scarcity statements without real awareness. We're not consciously saying, "Look, I ran the numbers for last month. We've got a twenty-seven percent budget shortfall, which leaves us insufficient cash flow for the Hawaii project." We're just knee-jerking a habitual "I can't afford it" because that's what we've *always* done. The phrases just pop out of our mouth by default—in fact, we've been saying them for so long we don't even *hear* them anymore.

This is a crucial insight. If our thoughts of scarcity and, as a result, our *words* of scarcity are habitual, then *scarcity itself is also habitual.*

In other words, the lack of abundance in your life isn't bad luck, or lack of smarts, or the wrong connections, or the lack of an education; your lack of abundance is a *habit.*

Second, scarcity statements are often untrue.

If you want to go to Hawaii, there's a good chance you actually *can* afford it. The truth is that you're afraid you won't be able to pay for something else—your car, your home, your bills.

But what if your *life* depended on you getting to Hawaii? What if your children's lives depended on you spending seven days in Waikiki? You'd surely find a way to afford it then. Why? Because when the stakes are high, you realize it's not about resources. It's about *resourcefulness*.

"I can't afford to go to Hawaii" is about resources. It's scarcity thinking. "I'm going to Hawaii next winter. How will I do it?" is resourcefulness. It's abundance thinking.

Be wary of scarcity statements masquerading as the truth.

Noticing your scarcity thinking

If thinking correctly is what creates the right action for abundance—if, in essence, the right thinking is what "gets you to Hawaii," then your goal is to become *more aware of your scarcity thinking* and shift it to abundance.

You can begin by noticing your thoughts and words. For example, if you hear yourself say, "There's never enough money to pay the bills," then ask yourself: *Did that thought come from a place of scarcity or abundance?*

You'll know immediately.

Now, reverse the thought. Substitute a new thought or phrase, such as "I always have enough" or "I'm choosing not to afford this right now."

Declare the new statement out loud from a place of abundance.

Habit vs. ritual

Because so much of scarcity thinking is habitual, it can be a challenge to build that initial awareness. You might read this right now and think, "Okay. I'm going to become more aware of scarcity thinking." But in moments, your habits can reactivate and you'll be thinking and saying the same things without being aware of it.

To begin lasting change, it can be helpful to develop *rituals* that you can use to replace your habits.

On the surface, rituals and habits may seem similar. You may think you have a morning ritual of waking up, making coffee, brushing your teeth, and reading the paper, but what you really have is a series of *habits*.

The difference is in the level of consciousness. A habit is unconscious. We do it without thinking. A ritual, on the other hand, is something that we do much more intentionally. We do it consciously, with purpose. As a result, rituals can be a tool to deliberately change our habitual thoughts, words, and actions toward complete awareness of what we're doing and why.

Here are three examples of rituals you can use to shift your scarcity mind-set toward one of abundance.

1. Go on a mental diet.

   The Seven Day Mental Diet by Emmet Fox talks about a conscious effort to become aware of negative thinking. For a week, your goal is to try not to sustain any negative thoughts. You may have them—we all do—but your job is to make a conscious effort to let them go, replacing them with something positive. Over time, this ritual can make you very aware of your scarcity thinking.

2. Develop a declaration ritual.

   I have a morning practice—a ritual—of several positive declarations that I make each day when I wake up. As soon as I put my feet on the floor, I begin with the statement, "I love my life." Then I continue with a series of positive declarations about the things I will experience that day, from gratitude and abundance, to love and joy.

   It's a conscious ritual that I do each morning and night. It takes just a few moments to complete, but it delivers every day, without fail.

3. Bless prosperity.

   In our culture, we have a habit of speaking negatively about the success of others. We might say, "He might be rich, but I bet he's unhappy" or "She only became rich by being greedy."

   Even though those statements may appear to be about others, we're really hurting ourselves when we make them. Tell yourself "money is the root of all evil" often enough and you'll believe it.

And then what will you think of *yourself* when you get some? When we make negative comments about the financial success of others, we're in effect *cursing ourselves*.

To end the curse, develop a ritual of *blessing* others who have prosperity. "She worked so hard for her money. I hope it brings her great joy." You can take this an extra step by making an effort to engage with those people, blessing the interaction, and being open to learning and receiving support from them.

At the heart of these rituals is a conscious decision about whether to focus on lack or abundance. Do you see prosperity as a pie with limited size, where some people get bigger slices and some get small? Or do you see it as limitless bounty of abundance?

The former is a scarcity mind-set and it's extremely common for that mind-set to be an unconscious habit. Ritual is about becoming aware and changing that unconscious choice so you can shift your mind-set to one of abundance.

The best part is that over time you'll notice something new: *Your conscious abundance rituals have become your new unconscious habits.* And that's where the magic happens.

3

Karmic Life and Business

WE TEND TO look at the world as made up of competitors. At work we compete for promotions, budgets, resources, and the ever-vaunted corner office. In business we compete for profits, attention, customers, contracts, and market share. Even in our home life, we compete for everything from the opportunity to be heard to the choice of where our next vacation will be.

It's no surprise that this is the case—after all, it's how we were raised. From an early age we were taught to win in sports, to "wrestle" with siblings for attention, and to strive for grades with our classmates. We've been programmed from day one to *compete.*

At the root, however, competition is fundamentally about scarcity. In fact, scarcity is the only way that competition can exist at all. If we saw everything as limitless, there would be no need to compete at all—the idea itself would seem absurd. But we haven't been programmed that way, and the result is that in everything from our home to our office, we inevitably build an us-versus-them competitive mind-set.

In the book *Karmic Management*, authors Geshe Michael Roach, Lama Christie McNally, and Michael Gordon turn this idea on its head, arguing that we should see everyone as our "karmic business partners," with our highest goal being not to ensure that we are successful, *but that they are.*

In this model, you look to collaborate, not compete. If you're in the microwave oven business, you don't try to corner the market, undercut the competition, or win the war for search engine results. Instead, you root for your competitors; you wish them well and even buy their products. You don't beat your vendors down on price; rather, you work with them collaboratively to find a way to ensure that they succeed. You don't try to squeeze the most work per dollar from an employee; instead, you work to make him or her as successful as possible so that the productivity will flow back to you.

You don't need to be an entrepreneur to reap the benefits of karmic management. As an employee, you can see your peers as karmic partners, too, not corner office competitors. You can help *them* get the promotions, the raises, and the kudos, and discover the wonder of watching it come back to you in turn.

If this sounds like "You get what you give" or "Do unto others," you're right. It is. But it's also more than that. Karma in life is about eliminating fear by acknowledging the abundance in the world and finally seeing the divine in everyone and everything around you.

A great example of how giving benefits the giver is Google, which in 2011 built physical community hubs or coworking spaces called *campuses*, where entrepreneurs come to learn, share ideas, and launch start-ups.

Google also supports and reaches out to minority-owned businesses to join its Accelerate with Google Academy, a free twelve-week program aimed at small-business owners who are looking to take their marketing to the next level and significantly grow their revenues using online advertising.

In a case of helping others to help themselves, Google shows businesses how to create website landing pages, manage Google AdWords to advertise their business, and manage marketing campaigns. The program is beneficial to businesses as well as to Google: More businesses using Google's services gives the search company more data to mine and helps it provide more granular data to people who are searching for businesses.

Here are six examples of things you can do to help others, your business, and yourself at the same time.

1. Connect with like-minded businesses. By joining forces, small businesses can achieve economies of scale and have a presence that can compete with larger corporations. There is power in the

collective, and businesses can harness the power of community to move forward.

2. Participate in your local chamber of commerce events, Meetup. com, and similar networks for interested parties in your area. Build a strong Twitter network so you can organize a tweetup to leverage that network into an even more powerful experience through face-to-face networking.

3. Join a social network or virtual group for like-minded small business owners to exchange advice, get support, build partnerships, find help, and more. For example, join Entrepreneur Connect, part of the Entrepreneur Network and Entrepreneur.com.

4. Build informal alliances with like-minded companies. Reach out to other companies who share your views on customer service, business, product development, etc. Start with simple steps like swapping guest posts or sharing online communities.

5. Create a "support small business" mind-set in your own company. Support your local economies by shopping at independently owned brick-and-mortar businesses. You can adopt a similar mind-set at your own business. Analyze your current vendors and service providers for opportunities to "downsize." Are there any places where you could be supporting a small business—virtual or physical?

6. American Express Open Forum online (https://www. americanexpress.com/us/small-business/openforum/articles/8-ways-small-businesses-help-communities-1/) is a great resource for small- and medium-sized businesses to help each other and to be visible to a much larger audience nationally and globally.

What to Do When Things Go Wrong

In your quest to find financial peace, things are inevitably not going to go as planned. It's nice to have a road map to follow, but if there's one thing you can count on, it's that not every road is going to be as smooth as you'd like.

A big part of the reason is that *you're going to make mistakes*. Money is going to flow into your life because of great decisions, but it's also going to flow back out because of some not-so-great ones. Some days you'll make decisions that earn you a windfall, and on others you'll make errors that cost a fortune.

And while the times you get everything right are wonderful, you'll never escape the downturns; inevitably, *you're going to screw up* and you're going to make a mistake that costs you. It may cost you in time, in energy, in heartache, or in cash, but whatever the cost, know that it will happen.

The issue, then, isn't *if* you'll make mistakes on the road to prosperity, but *what you'll do when they happen.*

First of all, know that you're not alone. Mistakes happen all the time, yes. But understand that *they happen to everyone*, not just you. You may have screwed up, but you haven't screwed up any worse than the rest of us. If it doesn't seem that way, it's because most people don't like to talk about failure. Show me someone with a perfect, error-free life and I'll show you someone who's too scared to tell you the truth.

With this in mind, you're presented with a glorious new opportunity the next time you make a mistake: *You don't have to beat yourself up the way you usually do.*

The greatest danger when things go wrong isn't the thing going wrong, but your judgment of yourself in the situation. You may judge yourself by feeling you caused the mistake. Or perpetuated it. Or weren't able to resolve it. You may judge yourself for your response to the hardship. But the cause, the response, the behavior, the resolution—they all matter less than *how you treat yourself in their wake.*

That's the real potential "wrongness" of being wrong.

This "failure phobia" we all experience is something we come by honestly. We all learned early that mistakes are "bad." You make a mistake on a test? You get a C instead of an A. You bring that C home? Your parents are upset. You make a mistake in the office? You could lose your job. Your career. Your license.

Our world punishes mistakes. That's the lesson you were taught, and it's why you take failure personally.

Ultimately, though, that perception is also what slows you down. It stops you from trying something new. From taking risks. From doing things that are intuitive. That failure phobia stops you from taking a moment to listen to that inner voice, the whisper of your soul, saying *Try something different.*

Yes, the programmed lessons of mistakes are powerful ones. Right now, you have many years of unconscious training telling you to ignore your instincts, your intuition, your *soul.* You have decades of programming telling you to invest your time and energy in just *maintaining.* In treading water. In protecting the status quo at all costs.

But remember the cost of that. It's *mediocrity.* A ceaseless, mindless commitment to what is *safe.*

Here's what you're telling yourself: *Mistakes are bad. I made one, so I must be bad, too. If I just never make another one, everything will be okay.*

But it won't, will it?

It's time to realize that mistakes are the best thing that could happen to us. Not in the trite sense of "everything happens for a reason," but in the knowledge that everything happens for a reason, and *that reason is there to serve.*

What to do when things go wrong? Forgive yourself, forgive others, and *find the reason that is there to serve.* Find the nugget of wisdom. The lesson. And move forward to something even better.

Don't avoid the mistakes because you're afraid you might be something less.

Celebrate the mistakes, because without them you just might be.

I have not failed. I've just found ten thousand ways that won't work.
—Thomas A. Edison

Just like Thomas Edison, who made more than ten thousand attempts before he found the proper substance to make the filament for the lightbulb, you too have found ways that won't work and you are on your way to inventing what will work to light your version of a lightbulb. And it will most likely take a lot less than ten thousand tries.

Hold On Lightly: Letting Go of Expectations

The root of suffering is attachment.
—Buddha

Expectation can be a heady, intoxicating feeling. Looking forward to that first date. Dreaming of your next vacation or your annual bonus. Picturing the new car you'll buy when your lease expires or the new home you'll move into after your wedding. They're all exciting plans for the future, and they carry an emotional charge that gives us a little boost of pleasure when we anticipate them.

On the surface, that seems pretty harmless. After all, what could be wrong with having something to look forward to?

The problem occurs when expectations grow into a powerful form of *attachment*, and that has some very real potential side effects.

Expectations have a way of evolving into a need to have things turn out in a very specific way. You get so caught up in exactly how you expect something to be that you can't accept anything different. You're attached to an outcome that's so specific—the perfect weather for your perfect wedding day—that you can't enjoy the real value of the moment.

Attachment also puts energy anywhere but in the present. It's a focus on the future—*this is where I'm going* or *someday I'll have that*. Or it's a focus on the past—*I'm not going back there again* or *I deserve better because of all that hard work*. As a result, attachment has a way of becoming like wearing a set of blinders: You can miss opportunities and possibilities that are just outside your narrow field of vision. When you're too attached, you simply can't see them.

So how, then, do we resolve the need to have goals for the future—to plan and set a course for where we want to be—with the dangers of attachment?

To start with, instead of goals, I prefer the term *intention*. In law *intent* is a big deal. When we look to where criminality lies—in determining first-degree or second-degree murder, for example—we rely on intent. Did the person *intend* to cause harm or was it accidental or negligent?

Intention is a powerful force in law and no less so in life. Where a goal is a wish, an intention is a declaration of the energy behind an outcome. Goals can be a slippery slope to attachment; intention, on the other hand, is about the energy of the present.

Once you have an intention, it's time to walk the tightrope. You need to set an intention, but then *let go of the outcome*—be willing to let go of your need to have things work out in a certain way. You must be willing to *detach*.

This can be a tricky idea. Detaching isn't about not caring. After all, how can you stay motivated to do what's required to move ahead in life if you don't care? What you're really detaching from is the *meaning* of things. Consider the following statements:

If I get the promotion, I'll be respected.
If I earn this much, I'll be happy.
If I have this and that, people will look up to me.

Those are all ways of attaching meaning to things and events, and it's that *meaning* that has the power to cause suffering. Detach from the meaning, and you detach from suffering the fear of a failed outcome.

Set the intention, but detach from the meaning. Accept that the outcome may be different, and the path impossible to see. Imagine that your intention is a beautiful rose that you hold in your hands. Hold it too loosely and you lose it. But hold it too tightly and you crush it.

The secret is to *hold on lightly*.

The Trim Tab Factor

In my midtwenties, before my pivot to life as an attorney, I was working in New York City as a public school teacher. My wife was a teacher, too, but working on Long Island.

During her time there she met a couple with a boat. We hit it off, and one weekend they invited us to go with them to Block Island—a trip of a hundred miles or so from Port Washington.

The boat was large enough and comfortable enough for the trip, but it was no cruise ship. We didn't have the radar you might find on a larger ship, but instead something called LORAN, a system of radio beacons and charts that could be used to navigate from waypoint to waypoint.

Our boat also had *trim tabs*—small steel planes that could be adjusted to keep the boat more level in the water. As I learned, changes in the angle of the boat in the water could not only make you more or less efficient, but over a long journey those changes could also have an effect on your path through the water and take you off your charted course.

Now, on a clear day, you can see Block Island from the mainland. It's not exactly an Atlantic crossing—no big deal at all on a clear day with calm weather. During our trip, however, a fog bank rolled in and we couldn't see much past the bow of the boat.

It's an unsettling experience to hit bad weather on the ocean. What seems incredibly benign and easy in one sunny moment can become quite threatening when the weather changes in the next. There we were in a twenty-seven-foot boat, unable to see *anything* and surrounded by a very, very big ocean. If we lost our way, we could run out of gas in the Atlantic, adrift to who knew where. Not an appealing prospect.

To complicate matters, the area was full of boat traffic, much of it a lot bigger than us. We certainly couldn't see them, and we couldn't count on them seeing us or even being able to adjust course in time if they could.

In short order, our pleasant sea voyage seemed to become very serious.

What if we lost our way or missed a waypoint? I knew that tiny mistakes in our direction could stack up and lead us many miles off course. Navigating accurately became priority number one, and part of that was a near-constant process of adjusting the trim tabs and tweaking the rudder and controls to make sure we traveled successfully from one waypoint to the next.

Of course, we made the trip just fine, but it has occurred to me many times since that life isn't so different. You make these small changes in your direction all the time, and over the course of months, then years, then decades, they have an *enormous* difference in where you arrive and when—it's the trim tab factor of life.

It's been said that *Apollo 11*, carrying Neil Armstrong and the rest of the first lunar crew, was "off course" for much of the journey. On a trip of a hundred miles on the Atlantic, that can mean missing your mark and heading into open ocean. On a mission of almost a *million* miles from the earth to the moon and back, missing your target and sailing off into the universe unchecked means you can end up . . . well, *infinitely* off course. Forever. It was only the work of readjusting the course that ensured they reached the moon safely.

In your financial life, the trim tabs tend to be your habits—the small things you do without fail. How you budget, save, spend. How you think and talk about money every day. As with our boat, small changes in direction can make a huge difference in where you end up financially. A little comment here and a few extra dollars there. They add up over time.

Do you constantly assess your position in life and adjust accordingly? Or do you drift aimlessly and run the risk of waking up a million metaphorical miles from where you hoped you'd be?

The above everyday events and stories illustrate and provide insights, tools, and lessons that transfer directly to your business and finances. As you progress in the book, you will find more stories, techniques, and inspiration that will help you achieve the abundance and success you are looking for.

PART TWO
Soul Over Matter

4

What Is Soul Over Matter?

I N RECENT DECADES, millions of people on Mother Earth have stud-ied and practiced *mind over matter*. "Mind over matter" means the mind can make things happen. The mind has power to improve health, heal sickness, transform relationships, improve finances, increase wisdom and intelligence, and bring success to every aspect of life. To practice mind over matter, you can meditate, make affirmations, apply positive thinking, do creative visualization, and communicate with the spiritual world, including Heaven, Mother Earth, the Divine, and Source. Many teachers have written many books and articles, given numerous lec-tures, and offered many workshops about mind over matter.

In our personal opinion, mind over matter is great. However, mind over matter is not enough. The next frontier is *soul over matter*. "Soul over matter" means the soul can make things happen. The soul has power to transform every aspect of life. In this book, we share the deep wisdom and practical techniques of soul over matter to create financial abundance.

Three Sacred Ancient Words to Transform Finances

Much ancient wisdom and practice focuses on three sacred words: jing, qi, and shen. "Jing" means *matter*. "Qi" (pronounced *chee*) means *energy*. "Shen" (pronounced *shun*) encompasses *soul, heart*, and *mind*. Everyone and everything is made of jing qi shen.

Einstein's formula of mass-energy equivalence, $E=mc^2$, explains the relationship between qi (E) and jing (m). However, Einstein's formula and his theories of special and general relativity do not include shen.

Your body, your systems, your organs, your cells, your DNA and RNA are made of jing qi shen. An animal is made of jing qi shen. A tree, a mountain, an ocean are made of jing qi shen. A city, a country, and Mother Earth are all made of jing qi shen. Mother Earth is one planet. There are countless planets, stars, galaxies, and universes. Each one is made of jing qi shen.

Let us explain *shen* further. Shen includes soul, heart, and mind. Mind means consciousness. There are all kinds of consciousness, including superficial consciousness, deep consciousness, and subconsciousness. A human being has a mind. Does an animal have a mind? Does a business have a mind? The heart is the core of life. Every aspect of life has this core. A human being has a heart, but the heart that is part of shen is more than the physical heart. Does a business have a heart? Does a business have a soul? Our answers are "Yes." Everyone and everything, including every business, has a mind, heart, and soul.

Soul is spirit. Quantum science talks about information or message. Digital physics posits that the physical world can be described by information. In fact, information or message is spirit. Spirit is soul. Spirit and soul are different terms for the same thing. Information or message are used in scientific study. Soul and spirit are used in spiritual study. They are the same. For centuries, scientists have sought a "theory of everything"—one set of universal principles and laws that can explain everything in the physical universe. We believe now is the time to unite the physical world and the spiritual world as one. Science and spirituality can meld as one if they can reach a common understanding of information and soul.

In summary, we emphasize that *everyone and everything is made of jing qi shen.* A human being's life has many aspects, including health, relationships, finances, career, intelligence, and family. Every aspect of life is made of jing qi shen. Finances and business are made of jing qi shen also. These three sacred ancient words, jing qi shen, carry incredible wisdom that can guide every reader, every businessperson, and every human being to achieve financial abundance. You need to understand the deep wisdom and practice of jing qi shen so that you can apply the sacred wisdom and techniques to create unlimited abundance. In this book, we are delighted to explain jing qi shen in depth to help you create financial abundance.

In order to help you understand jing qi shen, we will explain jing qi shen for health and for finances.

Four Sacred Phrases for Success in Every Aspect of Life

There are four sacred phrases that can guide you to transform your finances, health, relationships, and intelligence, and bring success to every aspect of your life:

1. qi dao xue dao
2. yi dao qi dao
3. xin dao yi dao
4. ling dao xin dao

Qi Dao Xue Dao

The first sacred phrase is *qi dao xue dao*. "Qi" means *vital energy* or *life force*. "Xue" means *blood*. "Dao" means *arrive*. "Qi dao xue dao" (pronounced *chee dow shooeh dow*) means *qi arrives, (then) blood arrives*. For five thousand years, this sacred phrase has been the key principle in traditional Chinese medicine for healing all kinds of sickness. Qi is energy. Blood is matter. *The Yellow Emperor's Internal Classic*, the authority book of traditional Chinese medicine, states, "qi xing xue xing, qi zhi xue ning." "Xing" means *flow* or *move*. "Zhi" means *obstruct* or *block*. "Ning" means *stagnation*. "Qi xing xue xing, qi zhi xue ning" (pronounced *chee shing shooeh shing, chee jr shooeh ning*) means: *If qi flows, blood flows. If qi is blocked, blood is stagnant*. In traditional Chinese medicine, all sickness is due to blockages of qi and blood.

Traditional Chinese medicine further states that all kinds of pain, all emotional imbalances (anger, depression, anxiety, worry, grief, sadness, fear, and more), all kinds of growths (cysts, tumors, cancer), all mental disorders, all trauma—and much more—are due to blocked qi and stagnant blood. Therefore, the relationship of qi and blood is vital for health. *Qi dao xue dao* is the key for healing all sickness in traditional Chinese medicine.

What does this have to do with your finances and business? Finances and businesses are also made of jing qi shen. The jing (matter) of your finances includes your cash, your bank, your accountant, your workplace, your superiors, your colleagues, your staff, your home, your vehicle, and more. The jing of a business is its infrastructure, including the customer service, finance, IT, and human resource teams, the equipment, technology, physical offices, and much more. To be successful, every business must have a strong jing component. Every business needs a strong infrastructure.

The qi (energy) of a business consists of its vital functions, including planning, marketing, communicating, controlling, organizing, inspiring, leading, coordinating, balancing, training, executing, delivering, and more. The qi of your finances includes the roles and responsibilities of your job, your financial responsibilities to raise your children and support your family, maintenance of your home and vehicle, your charitable contributions, your financial recordkeeping, your tax returns, and much more.

Qi dao xue dao teaches us that qi leads jing. In fact, qi is the boss of jing. Jing and qi are yin and yang. Many people understand ancient wisdom about yin and yang. They understand that yin and yang are two. They may not understand that yin and yang are also one. Yin and yang are complementary, interconnected, and interdependent. Qi and jing must work together to ensure the success of your business or finances.

Always remember the sacred phrase *qi dao xue dao*. This is the relationship of qi and jing. How can you apply this sacred wisdom to business? When you plan, market, control, organize, inspire, balance, execute, and more, spend three minutes to silently chant (say repeatedly) in your heart *qi dao xue dao* (pronounced *chee dow shooeh dow*). This chant gives a message to the qi of your business to lead and a message to the jing of your business to follow. Your qi will lead better and your jing will follow better. Affirming this message by chanting it could bring your business remarkable blessings.

Yi Dao Qi Dao

The second sacred phrase is *yi dao qi dao*. "Yi" means *consciousness*. Consciousness is *awareness, thinking, using the mind*. "Yi dao qi dao" (pronounced *ee dow chee dow*) means *thinking arrives, (then) energy arrives*. This is the relationship of the mind and qi. This is mind over matter.

Millions of people meditate to train the consciousness. *Yi dao qi dao* is the secret to meditation. When you focus your mind on an area of the body, energy will go there. For example, if you focus on your kundalini, which is in front of the sacrum and one of the body's most important energy centers, energy will go there. *Yi dao qi dao* is a one-sentence secret to train your consciousness. Mind leads energy. Mind is the boss of energy. When you focus your consciousness on some part of your business, energy will flow there and then matter will follow. Adam shared in his introduction, "Where attention goes, energy flows, and results show." This is the sacred process of *yi dao qi dao, qi dao xue dao*. These two sacred phrases teach us powerful sacred wisdom and practical techniques. They explain why mind over matter works. Mind drives energy and matter for your financial flourishing.

Xin Dao Yi Dao

The third sacred phrase is *xin dao yi dao*. "Xin" means *heart*. "Dao" means *arrive*. "Yi" means *consciousness*. "Xin dao yi dao" (pronounced *sheen dow ee dow*) means *heart arrives, (then) mind arrives*. This is the relationship, wisdom, and practice of the heart and mind. The heart is the core of life. The heart is the receiver of messages from the soul. The heart digests, absorbs, and passes the soul's messages to consciousness, which is mind. The heart leads consciousness. Mind is the processor. *Xin dao yi dao* tells us that the heart is the boss of consciousness. There is another ancient sacred phrase that expresses this beautifully: *xin xiang shi cheng*. "Xin" means *heart*. "Xiang" means *think*. "Shi" means *thing*. "Cheng" means *accomplish*. "Xin xiang shi cheng" (pronounced *sheen shyahng shr chung*) means *heart thinks, things can manifest*. This happens through the sacred process of *xin dao yi dao, yi dao qi dao, qi dao xue dao*. The heart leads mind, mind leads energy, energy leads matter.

Ancient wisdom also explains that *the heart houses the mind and soul*. To transform the heart is to transform the soul and mind. How does this apply to business? The key is to develop business from the heart and soul first; then pass it to the mind. To transform business and finances, purify and open the heart. Purify and open the heart of the business. Purify and open your heart. In chapter eight, we will give you practical techniques to remove blockages from the shen qi jing of every aspect of your business and finances to create unlimited abundance.

Ling Dao Xin Dao

The last sacred phrase is *ling dao xin dao*. "Ling" means *soul*, which is information or message. "Ling dao xin dao" (pronounced *ling dow sheen dow*) means *message arrives, (then) heart arrives*. To heal any sickness, use soul power to give a positive message that is loving, forgiving, compassionate, humble, and harmonious—with light and more. The same principle applies in business and finances. The message for business must be loving, clear, and serve a good purpose.

To summarize and further emphasize these four powerful sacred phrases:

Qi dao xue dao. *Energy arrives, blood arrives.* Energy is the boss of blood. Qi leads matter. If qi moves, physical material follows. *Qi dao xue dao* is the one-sentence secret for all healing in traditional Chinese medicine. We have just revealed that you can apply this secret to business and finances.

Yi dao qi dao. *Thinking arrives, energy arrives.* Thinking is consciousness. Thinking is the boss of qi. So, consciousness drives energy, and matter follows. Mind over matter is great. Yi dao qi dao is the one-sentence secret of mind over matter. It is the one-sentence secret for millions of people who meditate. It is also a one-sentence secret for businesses and finances. Consciousness drives energy. Energy drives material. Consciousness is important. But, in our opinion, consciousness is not enough. Mind over matter is not enough. We have to involve the heart and soul to truly transform business and finances. The root of success does not come from consciousness. *The root of success comes from the heart and soul.*

Xin dao yi dao. *Heart arrives, consciousness arrives.* The heart is the core of life. The heart is the receiver of the soul's messages. The heart directs consciousness. A human being has a heart. Every business, every relationship, and every aspect of life has its own heart. Do not think only of the physical heart of a human being. In chapter eight, we will lead you in some powerful practices to help you purify and transform your heart and the hearts of your finances and business. Purify your heart, purify the hearts of your finances and business, purify the heart of every aspect of your life. Success and flourishing are waiting for you and your finances and business.

Ling dao xin dao. *Soul* or *spirit arrives, heart arrives.* Soul is information or message. Soul is the boss of the heart. *Ling dao xin dao* is the one-sentence secret for all healing in Soul Mind Body Medicine.[1] The message must be clear and correct. If the message is not clear and correct, there is no way for you to be healthy. *Heal the soul first; then healing of the mind and body will follow.* Similarly, if the message is not clear and correct, there is no way for your finances or business to flourish. The soul is like the roots of a tree. If the roots are not healthy, the tree cannot be healthy.

Why do some people have successful businesses and abundant finances? Why do some companies flourish? In one sentence:

Great success in finances, business, and every aspect of life comes from *shen qi jing he yi*.

"He" means *join.* "Yi" means *one.* "Shen qi jing he yi" (pronounced *shun chee jing huh ee*) means *shen* (which includes soul, heart, and mind), *energy, and matter join as one.* This one-sentence secret is also profound ancient wisdom.

Why can't some businesses or some people's finances flourish? In one sentence:

Lack of success is due to shen qi jing not joining as one.

Why can't shen qi jing join as one? Because there are blockages in shen qi jing.

Jing blockages are blockages in the infrastructure of a business or finances. Investigate the weaknesses in your infrastructure, including your various department teams, equipment, technology, facilities, and more. Understand them and correct them.

---

[1] Zhi Gang Sha: *Soul Mind Body Medicine: A Complete Soul Healing System for Optimum Health and Vitality.* Novato: New World Library, 2006.

Qi blockages are blockages in the functions of a business, including planning, organizing, controlling, marketing, developing, strategizing, inspiring, communicating, coordinating, leading, executing, delivering, and much more. Find the weaknesses in your business' functions and correct them.

Shen blockages are the root blockages for a business and finances. Remember that shen includes soul, heart, and mind.

Mind blockages include negative mind-sets, negative beliefs, negative attitudes, ego, attachments, and more.

Heart blockages include impurities such as selfishness, greed, desire for fame or money, and more. Ancient wisdom summarizes heart blockages in three words: *tan* (greed), *chen* (anger), and *chi* (lack of wisdom in activities, speech, and thoughts).

Soul blockages are negative karma. Karma is the record of one's services in all lifetimes. Karma can be good (positive) or bad (negative). Two primary kinds of karma are personal karma and ancestral karma. Negative personal karma is created by a person's mistakes (hurtful or harmful actions and intentions) in this life and all previous lifetimes. Negative ancestral karma is created by the mistakes made by one's ancestors in all lifetimes.

If you and your business offer love, care, compassion, sincerity, honesty, generosity, kindness, purity, integrity, grace, and other kinds of good service to others, you and your business accumulate good karma. Heaven will give you and your business good virtue, which is spiritual currency that has the form of Heaven's flowers that are recorded in your book in the Akashic Records. The Akashic Records is an endless heavenly library where every soul's service is recorded. Your soul, your business' soul, and every soul has a book in the Akashic Records. Your service, your business' service—everyone's and everything's service, good and bad—is recorded in the Akashic Records. Think of the Akashic Records as the universal memory bank. Every action, every behavior, every utterance, and every thought are recorded there. Ancient wisdom says, "If you do not want people to know something, do not do it." Whatever you do, Heaven knows, Mother Earth knows, and you know.

If a person or a business serves well, Heaven gives a lot of virtue. This spiritual currency (in the form of bright and colorful heavenly flowers) is Heaven's reward for serving well. The virtue a person has earned in all lifetimes is the root cause for financial abundance, for good health, for good relationships, for high intelligence, and for success in every aspect of life.

If a person or a business offers unpleasant service to others, including killing, harming, taking advantage of others, cheating, stealing, and more, negative karma is created. This is recorded in the Akashic Records as dark, gray, and black flowers. The negative karma a person has accumulated is the root blockage that blocks finances, business, health, relationships, intelligence, and success in every aspect of life.

Karma can be summarized in one sentence:

Karma is the root cause of success and failure in every aspect of life, including health, relationships, and finances.

Soul Over Matter: The True Secret for Financial Abundance

For finances and business, soul over matter means the soul can create financial abundance. We have explained the ancient wisdom of jing qi shen. We have emphasized the four sacred phrases:

1. ling dao xin dao, *soul (message) arrives, heart arrives*
2. xin dao yi dao, *heart arrives, consciousness arrives*
3. yi dao qi dao, *consciousness arrives, energy arrives*
4. qi dao xue dao, *energy arrives, blood arrives*

Now we are ready to release the true secret for financial abundance. What is the real key for your finances and your business to flourish? In one sentence:

The root cause for financial abundance is one's good personal karma and good ancestral karma from all lifetimes.

This one-sentence secret has a flip side, a yin to this yang:

**The root cause for financial lack is one's negative personal karma
and negative ancestral karma from all lifetimes.**

Some people have great financial abundance. Some people find it impossible to achieve financial abundance. Many people wonder in their hearts, "Why does everyone have different financial abundance?" People are searching for the true and root cause of success. We have just revealed the true and root cause: good karma.

The key to creating financial abundance is to clear the root blockages of your finances, which are your negative personal and ancestral karma. In addition to clearing these soul blockages, you also need to clear heart, mind, energy, and matter blockages. At all times, create good karma to accumulate virtue. When the soul is clear, the heart, mind, energy, and matter can follow. The pathway of *soul over matter* will be smooth and successful.

In the next chapter, you will learn more sacred wisdom about karma. You will also learn practical techniques to remove jing qi shen blockages to create financial abundance.

5

Transform Your Finances and Business

THINK ABOUT HUMANITY. Many people on Mother Earth are very wealthy. Many people are very poor. A business owner in the Philippines once told me (Master Sha) he had a very good team. He also thought he planned and marketed well, but his business was not successful. He had a very close friend who did not plan or market much, but this friend's business decisions and business were always successful. The first business owner could not understand this at all.

Think about the people around you. Some people are very intelligent and capable. You might expect them to be very successful in business, but they may not be successful at all. Some people are very simple. They may even seem unintelligent, but they could be very successful.

In Toronto, I knew someone who made whatever business he touched very successful. He asked me, "Why am I such a very blessed person in business?" I paused a moment and did a spiritual reading by communicating with the Divine. I told him, "The Divine told me your success comes from your grandfather. Your grandfather did very good service for others, and this created lots of good virtue for him."

There is an ancient spiritual statement:

qian ren zai shu, hou ren cheng liang

"Qian ren" means *ancestors*. "Zai" means *plant*. "Shu" means *tree*. "Hou ren" means *descendants*. "Cheng liang" means *enjoy the shade*. Therefore, "Qian ren zai shu, hou ren cheng liang" (pronounced *chyen wren dzye shoo, hō wren chung lyahng*) means *ancestors plant the trees, descendants enjoy the shade*. If our ancestors have accumulated good virtue through good service to others, then we, their descendants, enjoy the benefits.

Let me continue the story of the businessman in Toronto. After hearing my spiritual reading, he was very surprised by its accuracy. He told me, "Master Sha, my grandfather was a spiritual leader. Thousands of people still follow his teaching. He was extremely loving, compassionate, and kind. People built statues and temples in our hometown to honor and remember him." This example tells us that because this man's grandfather gave great service to others, he enjoyed benefits and rewards in his business and finances.

Let me share another story from the renowned Chinese book of spiritual teaching *Liao-Fan's Four Lessons*, which was written in the early seventeenth century.

In Fujian Province, Rong Yang was prominent in the imperial court as the emperor's teacher. His ancestors were boat people who made a living by helping people cross the river.

One day, a storm caused severe flooding that washed away all of the houses in the area. People, animals, and possessions were swept downriver. Most of the boaters took advantage of the situation and collected the floating belongings for themselves. Only Rong Yang's grandfather and great-grandfather tried to rescue the people drowning in the river. They did not take any of the goods that floated by. All of the other boaters thought Rong Yang's grandfather and great-grandfather were very foolish.

After Rong Yang's father was born a short while later, the Yang family gradually became wealthy. One day a heavenly saint manifested as a Taoist monk and came to the Yang family to tell them that their ancestors, including Rong Yang's grandfather and great-grandfather, had accumulated much hidden virtue. Consequently, they and their descendants would enjoy prosperity and prominence. The monk also guided the family to build their ancestral tomb in a special place to honor and receive further blessings from their ancestors. They followed the monk's suggestion, and today this site is renowned as the White Hare Grave.

Rong Yang passed the imperial examination when he was only twenty years old. Later, he received an imperial appointment. The emperor granted the same imperial honors to Rong Yang's grandfather and great-grandfather. To this day, Rong Yang's many virtuous and prosperous descendants are still very prominent.

This is another great example of "ancestors plant the trees, descendants enjoy the shade." This is cause and effect. A good cause (action, behavior, or thought) brings good effects. The emperor honored Rong Yang's grandfather and great-grandfather for their service, which further benefited their descendants.

This story also reminds us to always remember to be kind to others. If you can serve, do it! Serve unconditionally, without any need or expectation of reward or recognition.

Why Some People Have Wealth

Why do some people have financial abundance? The root cause is good karma. They and their ancestors accumulated great virtue in their lifetimes. They served people very well. For this good service, they were given good virtue. This good virtue, which is recorded in the Akashic Records, has transformed to physical money in their current lifetimes. If they continue to serve well, they will continue to have financial abundance in future lifetimes. Their descendants will also flourish. The two stories I shared to begin this chapter are examples of this wisdom.

Why do other people struggle with poor financial conditions? The root cause is bad karma. They and their ancestors made significant mistakes in their lifetimes. Therefore, in order to transform your finances, the key is to clear your own bad karma and your ancestors' bad karma.

How can you clear bad karma? The best method can be summarized in one sentence:

To clear bad karma, offer unconditional universal service to humanity and Mother Earth.

Unconditional universal service is very important. However, it is very difficult to offer service that is truly unconditional. Many people think that if they offer some service, they should be paid. We are on Mother Earth. When someone offers professional service, he or she deserves to be paid. Everyone has to make a living. Everyone has responsibilities for the care of their families.

However, to self-clear negative karma, the key is to offer *unconditional* universal service. To offer unconditional service is to offer service without expecting anything in return. Just give pure service to others to make others happier and healthier.

There are many ways to offer unconditional service. For example, you can do volunteer work for a spiritual group, soup kitchen, homeless shelter, or school, donate to charity in time of natural disasters, and more. You can simply help people from your heart when they need assistance. I will discuss unconditional service further later in this chapter. The key is to understand that to offer this kind of service is to self-clear your negative karma. By offering good service, you are gaining virtue. This spiritual currency helps you repay your spiritual debt that accumulated because of your and your ancestors' negative karma.

Financial Abundance Can Be Lost

If you are wealthy but forget to offer service, or if you are not generous or kind to society or those who need support, then you could lose your virtue. Mother Earth is in a transition period. In recent years, many natural disasters have caused many people to suffer. If you are a wealthy person, have you donated money to relieve their suffering? You have the ability to do this. Do you do it? Nobody asks you to do it. If you do it, Heaven records your kindness and generosity. If you do not offer support, Heaven similarly records your lack of kindness. Remember, *everything* you have done is recorded in the Akashic Records, including your activities, behaviors, speech, intentions, and thoughts.

Some wealthy and powerful people may do unkind things. For example, a national leader may start a war in which many people are killed. This too is recorded in his or her book in the Akashic Records. Other government officials may implement policies that harm millions of people. This will create a record of very heavy bad karma. Some wealthy people take advantage of others, or get "dirty" money through gambling, cheating, or stealing. This also creates bad karma.

When a wealthy person creates bad karma, he or she loses virtue. Wealth in this lifetime is due to good service offered in previous lifetimes and this lifetime. For this good service, virtue was deposited into the person's virtue "bank account." If the person does unpleasant things in this lifetime, he or she will drain their virtue account.

It works just as it does in the physical world. One could have a large bank account. But if one continues to spend money without making new deposits, one day the account will have a zero balance or even a negative balance. A wealthy person who does unpleasant things continues to lose virtue, and his or her virtue account could reach a zero or negative balance.

Look at the economic conditions on Mother Earth now. Many companies have become bankrupt. Other companies have completely failed and disappeared. I will just offer a little reminder here: There is a spiritual reason behind any business or financial failure. Please be aware of this wisdom and think about it further.

Let me share more wisdom with you. Big businesses can have shareholders. Medium and small businesses can be owned by two or more partners. Take care in choosing your business partners. For example, if a business has ten major shareholders, and two or three of them have heavy bad karma, it will affect the entire organization. Please think a little more about this teaching also.

All of these examples and teachings are to share with you that a wealthy person must pay attention to karmic issues. The teachings can be summarized in one sentence:

A wealthy person who wants to maintain financial abundance must continue to offer good services.

Good services include offering unconditional love, forgiveness, compassion, generosity, kindness, purity, sincerity, honesty, integrity, and more.

The teaching has another side that can also be summarized in one sentence:

**A wealthy person who offers unpleasant services
could lose his or her business success and financial abundance.**

Unpleasant services include killing, harming, taking advantage of others, cheating, stealing, and more. Unpleasant services create bad karma. Bad karma can be created in many ways. Not many people really understand all of the types of bad karma. I am delighted to share the following teaching.

Types of Bad Karma

In ancient spiritual teaching, bad karma can be divided into three types: body karma, mouth karma, and thought karma.

- Body karma includes:
  - killing
  - stealing
  - cheating
  - physical abuse
  - sexual abuse
- Mouth karma includes:
  - lying
  - creating distrust and ill will between two parties
  - disrespecting
  - rudeness
  - criticizing
  - condemning
  - judging
  - complaining
- Thought karma includes:
  - greed
  - stinginess
  - anger
  - jealousy
  - wishful thinking (delusion)

To know more about the different kinds of bad karma from body, mouth, and thought is to remind yourself to avoid creating bad karma. If you realize you have issues with any of these three types of karma, you can be awakened and empowered to correct them. You also now know that if you do not correct your issues at the body, mouth, and thought levels, you will continue to create bad karma.

There is an ancient statement:

shan you shan bao, e you e bao

"Shan" means *kindness* and *good karma*. "You" means *has*. "Bao" means *return*. "E" means *harmfulness* and *bad karma*. "Shan you shan bao, e you e bao" (pronounced *shahn yō shahn bao, uh yō uh bao*) can be translated as *good karma returns, bad karma also returns*.

Good karma returns as good health, good relationships, and financial abundance, as well as blessings in every aspect of life.

Bad karma returns as sickness, challenging relationships, and poor finances, as well as blockages in every aspect of life.

How can you know whether you have good karma or bad karma? It is very easy to figure out. Are you healthy? Are your emotions balanced? Are your relationships blessed? Do your children behave well and get along with others? Do you have financial abundance? If you can answer *yes* to all of these questions, you definitely have very good karma from many lifetimes. If some of your answers are *no*, know that the root cause is bad karma. When you have special challenges in different aspects of life, especially if you find you face the same issues repeated over and over, that is very clearly a sign of bad karma and serious karmic lessons.

The important wisdom is that good karma and bad karma are what you and your ancestors have created. Now, in this moment and in every moment, you have the power to create karma for your future. If you want blessings for your health, relationships, and finances, offer good service. If you do not want karmic lessons for your health, relationships, and finances, stop creating bad karma from body, mouth, and thought.

This can be summarized in one sentence:

> **Create good karma with your ancestors and receive blessings;**
> **create bad karma with your ancestors and receive lessons.**

I wish that you will be careful not to create bad body karma, mouth karma, and thought karma. Every day, from the moment you awaken until the moment you fall asleep, discipline your activities, behaviors, words, intentions, and thoughts.

This is easy to say, but not always easy to do. Let me share a soul secret with you. If you do, say, or think something wrong, instantly say:

> *Dear Divine,*
> *I am sorry.*
> *Dear* _____ (name the persons you hurt or harmed),
> *I am sorry.*
> *Please forgive me.*

Then chant silently the Divine Soul Song *Love, Peace and Harmony*:

> *I love my heart and soul*
> *I love all humanity*
> *Join hearts and souls together*
> *Love, peace and harmony*
> *Love, peace and harmony*

The Divine Soul Song *Love, Peace and Harmony*[2] is a priceless divine treasure for self-clearing karma. It carries divine frequency and vibration with divine love, divine forgiveness, divine compassion, and divine light. Its power is beyond any words, comprehension, and imagination.

Why Some People Have Financial Challenges

The root cause of poor finances and all kinds of financial challenges is bad karma. In order to self-clear karma, remember the teaching above:

---

[2] I received the Divine Soul Song *Love, Peace and Harmony* from the Divine on September 10, 2005. To chant this Divine Soul Song is to self-clear negative karma. You can download a free mp3 file of *Love, Peace and Harmony* at www.LovePeaceHarmony.org.

If you have any issues of body karma, mouth karma, or thought karma, please be serious and disciplined to correct them.

There is only one way for you to self-clear karma: Offer good service. Make others happier and healthier. Help humanity and Mother Earth pass through this difficult time of transition and purification that is the result of our huge collective negative karma.

To offer good service is to create good karma. Creating good karma reduces your karmic debt. If you offer good service, virtue from Heaven's virtue bank is deposited to your virtue bank account in your Akashic Record book. This good virtue comes to you in the form of Heaven's flowers, which can be red, gold, rainbow, purple, crystal, or mixed colors. Virtue or Heaven's flowers are spiritual currency. This heavenly reward repays your karmic debt step by step. You must clear your karmic debt first. When this root blockage is removed, you will then have the possibility of seeing your finances flourish.

Virtue is yin money, which is currency in the spiritual world. Money on Mother Earth is yang money, which is currency in the physical world. Just as a human being needs money to spend in the physical world, a soul needs virtue to spend in the spiritual world.

The one-sentence secret about the relationship between spiritual money and physical money is:

**Virtue in the spiritual world can transform to
money in the physical world and vice versa.**

If you are wealthy, you have accumulated good virtue in previous lifetimes and in this lifetime. Some of this virtue has transformed to physical money in your present life. If you continue to serve well in this life, you will continue to accumulate good virtue. In future lifetimes, you could then continue to enjoy financial abundance. If you forget to serve, and especially if you go the opposite way and harm, take advantage of, cheat, or steal from others, you will create bad karma and lose virtue. You are spending the good virtue in your virtue bank account and could exhaust it.

If you lack physical money, you do not have much good virtue deposited in your Heaven's virtue bank account. In order to transform your finances, the key is to increase your virtue. To increase your good virtue, serve others unconditionally. The top secret to transforming finances and business is:

Offer unconditional universal service to transform your finances and business.

If you have heavy bad karma, it could take your greatest effort for many years or even many lifetimes to see significant improvement in your finances and business and to flourish in other aspects of life.

One day I was teaching a workshop in a church. A lady said, "Master Sha, I have served for more than twenty years. I have offered lots of volunteer support. I have served many friends, but I still have chronic health issues, relationship challenges, and financial hardship." I paused a moment. I checked directly with the leaders of the Akashic Records and the Divine. This person in all of her lifetimes had killed more than five hundred people. She carried huge bad karma.

I told her, "I am glad that you told me you have served for more than twenty years. What I can tell you is, if you had not served well for the past twenty years, the condition of your health, relationships, and finances could have been much worse."

She had an "aha!" moment then and totally accepted her condition because her soul understood her lives' records. Her heart got it also. She was grateful to receive this teaching.

I offered the teaching earlier in this chapter that major karma can be created from body, mouth, and thought. There is an ancient statement:

zhong sheng wei guo, pu sa wei yin

"Zhong sheng" means *ordinary beings*. "Wei" means *afraid*. "Guo" means *effect*. "Pu sa" means *bodhisattva*. "Yin" means *cause*. "Zhong sheng wei guo, pu sa wei yin" (pronounced *jōng shung way gwaw, poo sah way yeen*) means: *Ordinary beings are afraid of the effect, which includes sickness, broken relationships, and financial challenges, but a bodhisattva is afraid of the cause.* The cause is karma.

This teaches us to be afraid of karma. Why are bodhisattvas afraid of the cause? Because they understand that if you create bad karma, you must pay a price. Sometimes the price or effect will not happen until the next lifetime. For heavy bad karma, the price or effect could come for many lifetimes, one after another, for thirty, fifty, or even more than one hundred lifetimes. When the time comes, the effect could be very heavy, literally disastrous.

A bodhisattva is afraid of the cause, which is to create bad karma. A bodhisattva is an enlightened spiritual being whose main purpose is to become a buddha, a totally enlightened being. Creating bad karma will not only bring lessons to one's physical life, it will block a bodhisattva's spiritual journey.

Lao Zi, the author of the classic *Dao De Jing*, also wrote about karma:

huo fu wu men, wei ren zi zhao

"Huo" means *disasters*. "Fu" means *luck* or *blessings*. "Wu" means *no*. "Men" means *gate*. "Wei" means *only*. "Ren" means *human being*. "Zi" means *self*. "Zhao" means *attract*. "Huo fu wu men, wei ren zi zhao" (pronounced *hwaw foo woo mun, way wren dz jow*) means *there is no portal to one's disasters and blessings; a person attracts them all himself.*

This tells us that if you offer good service, good luck and blessings will come to you. If you offer bad service, lessons and disasters will come to you. It all depends on you. That is why it is important to discipline yourself in what you do (body), what you say (mouth), and what you think (thought). In this way, you will avoid creating bad karma and create only good karma.

When you do, say, or think something wrong, that is okay. The important thing is to correct your mistakes instantly. As I shared with you earlier, apologize to the Divine and to the person or persons you hurt or harmed. Sincerely apologize and transform the wrong action, speech, or thought instantly. Always remember to purify your soul, heart, mind, and body. Always improve yourself in what you do, what you say, and what you think. If you are consciously aware of this, then you can make rapid progress on your spiritual journey. When you avoid creating bad karma and create a lot of good karma, transformation of your finances and every aspect of life will follow. If you follow the teaching here and practice seriously, the benefits for your life can be unlimited. I wish you will really put this teaching into practice.

6

Create Good Karma to Transform Your Finances

HOW CAN YOU create good karma? You have learned that bad karma can be created from body, mouth, and thought. Good karma can also be created from body, mouth, and thought.

Another ancient spiritual statement teaches us how to create good mouth karma:

hua you san shuo, qiao shuo wei miao

"Hua" means *speech*. "You" means *has*. "San" means *three*. "Shuo" means *speak*. "Qiao" means *proper* or *artful*. "Wei" means *is*. "Miao" means *profound*.

"Hua you san shuo, qiao shuo wei miao" (pronounced *hwah yō sahn shwaw, chee-yow shwaw way mee-yow*) means *there are three ways to say something; the artful way is profound.*

Speaking has two sides, like yin and yang. You can speak properly and well or you can speak improperly and not well. Think about your daily life with family, at work, or in social gatherings. If you speak properly, with love, care, and compassion, you could make people happy, inspire them, and move and touch their hearts. You create good karma. If you speak improperly, rudely, or disrespectfully, you could make people upset or sad. You create bad karma.

49

The wisdom of creating good karma is:

To create good karma is to have good action, speech, and thought.

Are You Creating Good Karma or Bad Karma?

It is easy to understand how good and bad karma are created. Think again about your daily life. On some days you are very happy and loving. You speak with kindness and respect and treat others well. You are creating good karma. On other days you are irritated and upset. You could speak rudely and disrespectfully and treat others badly. You are creating bad karma.

Every time you do something, every time you speak something, every time you think something, always remember one principle: Are you serving only yourself or are you serving others by making them happier and healthier?

Good karma and bad karma are opposites. In one day, you can create good karma and accumulate virtue, Heaven's colorful flowers in your Akashic Record book. In the same day, you can create bad karma and accumulate gray or black flowers in your Akashic Record book. Gray or black flowers are given as records of unpleasant services, including killing, harming, taking advantage of others, cheating, stealing, and more. If you create bad karma, gray and black flowers will be added to your book in the Akashic Records, and some good flowers, which could be red, golden, rainbow, purple, or crystal flowers, will be removed.

Good flowers are given to reward a person with good health, good relationships, abundant finances, and more. Dark flowers are given to teach a person lessons, such as sickness, broken relationships, financial challenges, and more.

How do you know whether you are creating good karma or bad karma? Let me share a one-sentence secret about creating bad karma:

If what you do, what you speak, and what you think benefit only yourself, you are creating bad karma.

In every aspect of your life, apply this "ruler" to measure what you do, what you speak, and what you think. You will avoid creating bad karma. You will create good karma. The transformation in your life could be beyond imagination.

Now let me (Master Sha) explain further how to create good karma. Here is a one-sentence secret about creating good karma:

The best way to create good karma is to offer unconditional universal service through every aspect of your life.

To create good karma, first purify your heart. The heart houses the mind and soul. To purify your soul, heart, mind, and body in every aspect of your life, follow this key principle:

Create good karma by making others happier and healthier by what you do, what you speak, and what you think.

In one word, this principle for creating all kinds of good karma is *selflessness*. If everything you do, speak, and think is only for you, this is *selfishness*. Selfishness creates bad karma. In summary, the complete one-sentence secret for creating good karma and bad karma is:

**Selfishness creates bad karma;
selflessness creates good karma.**

In everything you do, speak, and think, always remember love, forgiveness, care, compassion, sincerity, honesty, purity, integrity, humility, generosity, and kindness. These are the standards for your actions, speech, and thoughts.

Good karma and bad karma are yin and yang. Your actions, speech, and thoughts fall either on the yang side or the yin side. If you are not going to yang, you are going to yin. If you are not going to yin, you are going to yang. Each action, speech, and thought is recorded in your book in the Akashic Records. Each action, speech, or thought will create either good karma or bad karma.

For speech, do you speak with kindness, love, forgiveness, compassion, and integrity? Do you speak with sincerity and honesty? Or do you speak rudely? Do you complain? Do you lie? Are you irritated or even angry?

An important ancient spiritual teaching is:

Anger burns good virtue.

If two people are arguing and one person is shouting and yelling while the other person is quiet, the person who is yelling is literally throwing his or her good virtue to the person who is quiet. The yelling person loses virtue. If both people yell at each other, then they are throwing virtue back and forth to each other.

For thought, do you think positively, lovingly, kindly, and generously? Or do you think negatively or angrily? Do you think of ways to hurt or take advantage of others?

For action, have you ever killed anything? Killing animals is considered killing. If, for example, you order live seafood at a restaurant, this is considered killing. You may not realize that it creates bad karma.

Let's focus on more ways to create good karma:

- donate to the poor
- build homes, schools, and hospitals
- support proper spiritual organizations and teachers with time or money
- serve world peace through various organizations, movements, and activities
- serve the elderly, the sick, the homeless, and others who suffer
- serve those who have suffered from an accident or disaster
- support organizations or individuals who offer kindness and service to others
- help and empower others to succeed
- heal others physically, emotionally, mentally, and spiritually
- teach others to heal themselves
- teach others to practice kindness, love, care, forgiveness, and compassion

- develop public projects for the greater benefit of people and society
- respect everyone
- love and cherish all beings, creatures, and things

To summarize the what, why, and how of one's financial condition:

- Wealth is due to good karma from past lifetimes and this lifetime.
- A wealthy person who continues to offer good service to humanity will continue to enjoy financial abundance in this life and future lifetimes.
- A wealthy person who creates bad karma could lose his or her financial abundance.
- Financial challenges are due to bad karma from past lifetimes and this lifetime.
- Financial challenges can be transformed by creating good karma through unconditional universal service.
- To create good karma is to earn good virtue and receive Heaven's flowers, which are spiritual currency. Spiritual currency in the spiritual world can transform to money in the physical world.

To summarize all of the above further, in one sentence:

**Transform the spiritual virtue bank account first;
then transformation of the physical bank account will follow.**

This teaching can be explained in another way. If you have financial challenges, the root cause is bad karma. In order to transform your finances, you must clear bad karma. How? In one sentence:

**Offer unconditional universal service to make others happier and
healthier through your good actions,
kind speech, and compassionate thoughts.**

To offer service is to gain virtue in your virtue bank account in the spiritual world. If you do not have enough physical money, you do not have enough virtue deposited in your virtue account. Spiritual virtue can be transformed to physical money. In order to transform your financial condition to gain money, transform your virtue bank account first. Gain good virtue first. If you have virtue, which is yin money, it can be transformed to yang money in the physical world.

This is the way for you and everyone to transform finances. Transform your virtue bank account first; then transformation of your physical bank account will follow.

I emphasize again that to serve is to self-clear bad karma because virtue, which is spiritual currency, is given as a reward for service. Bad karma creates spiritual debt. Virtue pays your spiritual debt. Pay your spiritual debt first, and then continue to serve. More virtue will then be given. Virtue—spiritual currency—will transform to physical money. Transform the virtue bank account first; then transformation of the physical bank account will follow.

Transform Your Finances with the Divine Soul Song *Love, Peace and Harmony*

One of the most powerful spiritual methods for transforming your finances is to sing the Divine Soul Song *Love, Peace and Harmony*. I received this song directly from the Divine on September 10, 2005. This Divine Soul Song carries power beyond comprehension:

- To chant or sing *Love, Peace and Harmony* is to serve. To serve is to gain virtue. Virtue will pay your spiritual debt.
- To chant or sing *Love, Peace and Harmony* is to heal your spiritual, mental, emotional, and physical bodies.
- To chant or sing *Love, Peace and Harmony* is to prevent all sicknesses.
- To chant or sing *Love, Peace and Harmony* is to purify your soul, heart, mind, and body.
- To chant or sing *Love, Peace and Harmony* is to rejuvenate your soul, heart, mind, and body.

- To chant or sing *Love, Peace and Harmony* is to clear your negative financial karma.
- To chant or sing *Love, Peace and Harmony* is to gain more virtue to transform your finances and business.

How does this Divine Soul Song work? When you chant or sing *Love, Peace and Harmony*, divine frequency and vibration with divine love, forgiveness, compassion, and light radiate to all humanity, all souls on Mother Earth, and all souls in all universes. The divine frequency of this Divine Soul Song is beyond imagination. In one sentence:

To chant or sing *Love, Peace and Harmony* is to apply divine transformation to your finances, business, and every aspect of life.

The following *Divine Soul Song for World Soul Healing, Peace and Enlightenment*, which I received in 2008, explains the power and significance of chanting *Love, Peace and Harmony* and other Divine Soul Songs:

Chanting chanting chanting
Divine chanting is healing
Chanting chanting chanting
Divine chanting is rejuvenating

Singing singing singing
Divine singing is transforming
Singing singing singing
Divine singing is enlightening

Humanity is waiting for divine chanting
All souls are waiting for divine singing
Divine chanting removes all blockages
Divine singing brings inner joy

Divine is chanting and singing
Humanity and all souls are nourishing
Humanity and all souls are chanting and singing

World love, peace, and harmony are coming
World love, peace, and harmony are coming
World love, peace, and harmony are coming

Mother Earth is in a great transition now. Humanity and Mother Earth are facing many challenges. Financial challenges are one of the major challenges for people, businesses, countries, and more. As I have explained, the root cause of financial challenges on Mother Earth is bad karma. Humanity has created heavy negative karma through killing, harming, and taking advantage of others, as well as by damaging Mother Earth. This bad karma is the root cause of the present financial challenges on Mother Earth.

It is very important for us to gather millions of people to apply divine transformation to transform finances and businesses on Mother Earth. If millions of people were to sing Divine Soul Songs and practice and chant with Divine Soul Mind Body Transplants (see the next section in this chapter)—all of which carry divine frequency and vibration with divine love, forgiveness, compassion, and light—the bad karma underlying the financial challenges on Mother Earth could be cleared. It would help transform finances on Mother Earth greatly. However, it does take time to transform heavy karma, whether for a person, a business, a country, or all of Mother Earth.

Let us sing the Divine Soul Song *Love, Peace and Harmony* together now to serve to transform finances and more on Mother Earth and beyond. Apply soul over matter. Say *hello*[3] first:

Dear soul mind body of humanity and all souls in all universes,
I love you, honor you, and appreciate you.
Let us sing the Divine Soul Song Love, Peace and Harmony *together.*

Lu La Lu La Li
Lu La Lu La La Li
Lu La Lu La Li Lu La

---

[3] The essence of soul over matter is Soul Power, one of the Four Power Techniques that I will explain later in this chapter. Soul Power is "Say Hello Healing and Blessing" by addressing souls and making a request of them for good service.

Lu La Li Lu La
Lu La Li Lu La

I love my heart and soul
I love all humanity
Join hearts and souls together
Love, peace and harmony
Love, peace and harmony

You can download the *Love, Peace and Harmony* song and lyrics in many languages for free on our website www.LovePeaceHarmony.org.

I have a wonderful story about *Love, Peace and Harmony*. At the end of 2009, I was teaching in the Netherlands. One night some students and I arrived at a restaurant at 9:15 pm. The owners explained to us that it was too late for us to dine there because they closed at 9:30 pm. However, after we spoke with them for a minute or two, they were very kind to cook for us. The meal was delicious.

The next day, I returned to the restaurant and told the owners, "Thank you very much for your kindness and delicious food last night. I would like to give you this CD of the Divine Soul Song *Love, Peace and Harmony* to bless your business." I had seen that the restaurant had only a few customers the night before and also that day. I explained to the owners that the Divine Soul Song *Love, Peace and Harmony* carries divine frequency and vibration with divine love, forgiveness, compassion, and light, and so it could clear the shen qi jing blockages of the restaurant's business and transform the business. The owners began to play the CD right away in the restaurant. I told them to play the CD continuously.

On the third day, I went to the restaurant again. It was filled with customers. The owners said, "This is amazing. Usually there are only a few customers here every night." At that moment, more than thirty diners were packed into the small restaurant.

On the fourth day, we went back. The restaurant was completely packed again. On the fifth day, the owners offered my team members a free dinner. They said, "This is absolutely amazing."

This story shows the power and ability of the Divine Soul Song *Love, Peace and Harmony* to transform a business almost instantly with divine frequency and vibration that carries divine love, forgiveness, compassion, and light.

In some cases, it will take more time to transform your finances, but this is divine transformation in action. Learn and practice this absolutely breakthrough method of divine transformation. It is extremely simple and practical. You have the power to self-clear negative karma. You have the power to transform your finances and business. But remember, if you have heavy negative financial or business karma, it takes time to see results. It could take many years to self-clear heavy negative karma.

Be patient and confident.

Practice. Practice. Practice.

Serve. Serve. Serve.

Self-Clear Your Negative Karma (Soul Blockages), Mind Blockages, and Body Blockages for Finances and Business

If you have financial challenges, the root cause is bad karma. The keys to self-clear karma are love and forgiveness. In this section, you will receive love and forgiveness in a very special way. Then I will lead you to practice with the special love and special forgiveness you are about to receive.

You will receive two major treasures, one of love and one of forgiveness, as a gift from Heaven. We will then apply these heavenly treasures to clear soul mind body (shen qi jing) blockages in your finances and business. These permanent soul treasures are named:

**Tao Rainbow Light Ball and Rainbow Liquid Spring of Tao Love
Soul Mind Body Transplants
and
Tao Rainbow Light Ball and Rainbow Liquid Spring of Tao
Forgiveness
Soul Mind Body Transplants**

My books are unique. The Divine and Tao (Source) "download" (transmit) their priceless permanent soul treasures to readers as they read these books. In the ten books of my Soul Power Series and the two books of my Soul Healing Miracles Series, the Divine and Tao have pre-programmed permanent soul treasures, which are Soul Mind Body Transplants, as gifts to readers. I will continue to offer this divine service in this book.

How do you receive these priceless treasures? Simply relax and continue to read. When you come to the appropriate paragraphs in the next pages, pause for a minute and Tao (Source) will transmit the Soul Mind Body Transplants named above to your soul. These treasures are rainbow light souls that come to your crown chakra, which rests on the top of your head, and move down through your Soul Houses[4] to reside in your lower abdomen.

After you receive the two permanent Tao treasures, I will immediately show you how to invoke them to offer healing, blessing, and transformation to any part of your body or any aspect of your life, including your finances and business.

Now let me offer the first set of priceless permanent Tao soul treasures to you.

Prepare! Sit up straight. Totally relax. Put both palms on your lower abdomen.

Tao Rainbow Light Ball and Rainbow Liquid Spring of
Tao Love Soul Mind Body Transplants
Transmission!

What are Soul Mind Body Transplants? They are three special souls (messages) created in the heart of the Divine or Tao (Source).

The Tao Love Soul Transplant is the soul of Tao love.

The Tao Love Mind Transplant is the consciousness of Tao love.

The Tao Love Body Transplant is the energy and tiny matter of Tao love.

Congratulations! You have received the shen qi jing of Tao love.

---

[4] There are seven houses of the soul in a human being. They are located in a vertical column in the center of the body, from the bottom of the torso (first Soul House or root chakra) to atop the head (seventh Soul House or crown chakra) and correspond to the seven major energy chakras.

Love melts all blockages and transforms all life.

Now I will offer the second set of priceless permanent Tao soul treasures as a gift to every reader.

Prepare! Sit up straight. Totally relax. Put both palms on your lower abdomen.

Tao Rainbow Light Ball and Rainbow Liquid Spring of Tao Forgiveness Soul Mind Body Transplants Transmission!

The Tao Forgiveness Soul Transplant is the soul of Tao forgiveness.

The Tao Forgiveness Mind Transplant is the consciousness of Tao forgiveness.

The Tao Forgiveness Body Transplant is the energy and tiny matter of Tao forgiveness.

Congratulations! You have received the shen qi jing of Tao forgiveness. Forgiveness brings inner joy and inner peace.

These Tao treasures are priceless. They could bring abundance to your finances and business, as well as flourishing to every aspect of life, beyond your comprehension. They are permanent gifts that will be with your soul forever.

Now let me show you how to apply your new permanent soul treasures to remove jing qi shen blockages from your finances and business. Love melts all blockages and transforms all life. Forgiveness brings inner joy and inner peace to all life. Love and forgiveness are the golden keys to transform all life, including finances and business.

Let us apply the Four Power Techniques with Tao Love and Tao Forgiveness treasures now:

Body Power. Sit up straight. Put your left palm over your Message Center or heart chakra[5] and your right hand in the traditional prayer position

---

[5] The Message Center is a fist-sized energy and soul center located in the center of your chest, behind the sternum. The Message Center is the love center, forgiveness center, karma center, healing center, life transformation center, soul enlightenment center, and more.

with fingers pointing upward. This is the Soul Light Era[6] Universal Service Hand Position. See figure 1.

Figure 1. Soul Light Era Universal Service Hand Position

Soul Power. Say *hello*:

> *Dear soul mind body of my finances and business,* _____ (if you have a business, state its name),
> *I love you, honor you, and appreciate you.*
> *You have the power to remove your soul mind body blockages.*
> *Dear Tao Rainbow Light Ball and Rainbow Liquid Spring of Tao Love and Tao Forgiveness Soul Mind Body Transplants,*
> *I love you, honor you, and appreciate you.*
> *You have the power to offer Tao love and forgiveness for the mistakes I, my ancestors, and my business' soul have made in past lifetimes and this lifetime.*

---

[6] The Soul Light Era began on August 8, 2003. It will last fifteen thousand years. In the Soul Light Era, *soul over matter* will play *the* vital role to heal, rejuvenate, and transform all life.

Dear all the souls that I, my ancestors, and my business' soul have hurt,
   harmed, or taken advantage of in past lifetimes and this lifetime,
Please come.
I sincerely apologize for all of the mistakes that we have made.
Please forgive us.
I have learned my lessons.
I will be a better servant for humanity.
Dear Tao Rainbow Light Ball and Rainbow Liquid Spring of Tao Love
   and Tao Forgiveness Soul Mind Body Transplants,
Please forgive me, my ancestors, and my business' soul for all our
   mistakes in all lifetimes.
I am very grateful.
I cannot thank you enough.

Mind Power. Visualize Tao light, with Tao love and Tao forgiveness, radiating in your business and finances.

Sound Power. Chant silently or aloud:

Tao Rainbow Light Ball and Rainbow Liquid Spring of Tao Love
   and Tao Forgiveness Soul Mind Body Transplants clear soul mind
   body blockages of my finances and business.
All souls that I, my ancestors, and my business' soul have harmed in
   all lifetimes, please forgive us.
Thank you, everyone.

Tao Rainbow Light Ball and Rainbow Liquid Spring of Tao Love and
   Tao Forgiveness Soul Mind Body Transplants clear soul mind body
   blockages of my finances and business.
All souls that I, my ancestors, and my business' soul have harmed in
   all lifetimes, please forgive us.
Thank you, everyone.

Tao Rainbow Light Ball and Rainbow Liquid Spring of Tao Love and
   Tao Forgiveness Soul Mind Body Transplants clear soul mind body
   blockages of my finances and business.

*All souls that I, my ancestors, and my business' soul have harmed in
    all lifetimes, please forgive us.*
Thank you, everyone.

*Tao Rainbow Light Ball and Rainbow Liquid Spring of Tao Love and
    Tao Forgiveness Soul Mind Body Transplants clear soul mind body
    blockages of my finances and business.*
*All souls that I, my ancestors, and my business' soul have harmed in
    all lifetimes, please forgive us.*
Thank you, everyone.

Next, chant repeatedly:

Love, love, love
Love, love, love
Love, love, love
Love, love, love
Love, love, love
Love, love, love
Love, love, love

Forgiveness, forgiveness, forgiveness
Forgiveness, forgiveness, forgiveness
Forgiveness, forgiveness, forgiveness
Forgiveness, forgiveness, forgiveness
Forgiveness, forgiveness, forgiveness
Forgiveness, forgiveness, forgiveness
Forgiveness, forgiveness, forgiveness

Peace, peace, peace
Peace, peace, peace
Peace, peace, peace
Peace, peace, peace
Peace, peace, peace
Peace, peace, peace
Peace, peace, peace

Success, success, success
Success, success, success
Success, success, success
Success, success, success
Success, success, success
Success, success, success
Success, success, success . . .

Close. After chanting for at least three minutes, close:

Hao! Hao! Hao!
Thank you. Thank you. Thank you.[7]

There is a renowned phrase in ancient sacred spiritual teaching:

Da Tao zhi jian

"Da" means *big*. Tao is the Source and Creator. Tao is the universal principles and laws that govern everyone and everything in all universes. Tao is The Way of all life. "Zhi" means *extremely*. "Jian" means *simple*. "Da Tao zhi jian" (pronounced *dah dow jr jyen*) means *the Big Way is extremely simple*. This book follows this principle. The practice we just concluded follows this principle. You could realize its simplicity very quickly. You could receive great transformation very quickly and wonder *how* and *why*.

I am humbled to co-create this book for humanity. I cannot thank Tao (Source), the Divine, and all Heaven's Committees enough for their sacred wisdom, knowledge, and practical techniques, as well as for their immeasurable power to bless us. How blessed humanity is that Source puts Source power in this book and offers permanent downloads as gifts to my readers. I am simply a servant and vessel for my readers, humanity, and all souls.

---

[7] "Hao" (pronounced *how*) means *good* or *get well* in Chinese. The first *thank you* is to the Divine, Tao, and your Tao Soul Mind Body Transplants. The second *thank you* is to all the souls who joined you. The third *thank you* is to your own soul, heart, mind, and body.

There is a one-sentence secret about chanting:

What you chant is what you become.

To chant *love, love, love, forgiveness, forgiveness, forgiveness, peace, peace, peace, success, success, success* is extremely simple. You may not realize the power of this simple soul practice. You may find it difficult to believe. This simple chanting practice is powerful beyond any words, comprehension, and imagination.

How should you practice and chant? Stop reading. Close your eyes. Chant from the bottom of your heart. You can chant silently or aloud. Sincerity and honesty are key. Sincerely practice love and forgiveness. Offer your total love and forgiveness. *Be* total love and forgiveness.

Sincerity and honesty move Heaven. The souls that you, your ancestors, and your business' soul have harmed can feel the sincerity and honesty of your true apology. Most of the souls that you harmed will forgive you. Some souls may not forgive you right away because they were harmed so badly. They may not forgive you easily. Therefore, you need to do this practice repeatedly and chant more.

Trust the sacred teaching here. Love and forgiveness are the golden keys to removing all blockages in every aspect of life. I started to teach love and forgiveness practices in 2002. Since then, I have received thousands of heart-touching and moving stories about the power and benefits of these practices. Love and forgiveness practices will bring millions of heart-touching and moving stories to humanity, Mother Earth, and all universes.

Love and forgiveness practices are practical spiritual treasures for transforming finances and every aspect of life.

Practice. Practice. Practice.

Experience. Experience. Experience.

Benefit. Benefit. Benefit.

Self-clear karma. Self-clear karma. Self-clear karma.

Transform finances and business. Transform finances and business. Transform finances and business.

Transform every aspect of life. Transform every aspect of life. Transform every aspect of life.

The Importance of the Name of a Business

Every human being has a soul. Every animal has a soul. Every business has a soul. Every business' name has a soul. Every word has a soul.

The name of your business is a message and a soul that can carry and create karma, positive or negative. Every name carries a message. When I lived in the countryside in China, quite a few parents gave the nickname *zhu er* to their sons. "Zhu" means *pig*. "Er" means *son*. They kept calling their sons *pig son*. It was intended to be a term of affection and endearment, but it deeply affected the intelligence of these children.

Therefore, choose a name for your business very carefully. If you choose a negative name for your business, your business could be deeply affected. Before you decide on your business' name, I suggest that you consult with a high-level spiritual being for a spiritual reading. It could really help you find the proper name for your business. The proper name will have good karma. The proper name will create more good karma.

Pay great attention to this spiritual wisdom. Pay great attention to your business' name. Choose it wisely for your business and finances to flourish.

Follow the Tao of Business

Many business experts have written many books and led many seminars and workshops to teach people how to be successful in various aspects of business. I am not a business expert, but I understand that for success in any aspect of life, it is vital to:

- remove the negative karma (soul blockages), mind blockages, and body blockages to success
- follow the Xiao Tao (the *small Tao*, pronounced *shee-yow dow*) of that aspect of life, which could be sleeping, eating, dressing, speaking, studying, or running a business

For success in business, it is vital to:

- clear the soul mind body blockages of your business, including finding a proper business name
- clear the soul mind body blockages of the relationships among all the employees and managers
- follow the Xiao Tao of business, which are the important fundamental principles for any successful business. The Xiao Tao of business includes:
  - a clear mission and goals
  - products and services that offer good service to humanity and Mother Earth
  - great leadership
  - effective communication
  - harmonized teamwork
  - efficient infrastructure
  - good planning
  - powerful marketing
  - proper financial and other controls
  - great customer service
  - avoiding greed and other unpleasant services

Follow the Tao of business. Your business and all of its team members will flourish.

You can learn many things about business leadership, planning, marketing, operations, and more from many books, seminars, and workshops. You could get help from a business expert or consultant. Business is business. You need to study and apply the proper ways to deal with all aspects of business.

What I can contribute to your business success is the spiritual wisdom, Tao treasures, and practical techniques that I have shared. In the next chapter, I will share a spiritual secret that I introduced in the authoritative book of my Soul Power Series, *The Power of Soul*.[8] It is soul marketing. I am honored to give the essence to you and humanity in this book.

---

[8] Zhi Gang Sha: *The Power of Soul: The Way to Heal, Rejuvenate, Transform, and Enlighten All Life.* Toronto/New York: Heaven's Library/Atria Books, 2009.

7

The Power and Significance of Soul Marketing

EVERY BUSINESS NEEDS marketing. Very successful businesses usually have great marketing strategies. Marketing is generally done through advertising, press releases, public relations, special promotions, and more. Marketing uses various media, including newspapers, magazines, websites, radio, television, email, flyers, posters, e-postcards, and more. In the last decade, social media marketing has emerged as a major marketing force, via Facebook, Twitter, YouTube, Instagram, Meetup, and more.

What Is Soul Marketing?

What I (Master Sha) am sharing now is *soul marketing*, which very few companies and people have heard of. Soul marketing is divine wisdom. **Soul marketing is to market to the soul.**

How many people are in your company?

How many people are in your city?

How many people are in your country?

How many people are on Mother Earth? There are currently about 7.4 billion human beings on Mother Earth. Every human being has a soul.

How many souls are in countless planets, stars, galaxies, and universes? There are countless souls.

In one sentence:

**Soul marketing is to market to all souls of humanity
and all souls in countless planets, stars, galaxies, and universes.**

Physical marketing has its limitations. Soul marketing has no limitations. Physical marketing is still important, but soul marketing has much greater reach and penetration than any physical marketing.

Every human being has a soul. Every organization has a soul. Every website has a soul. Every city has a soul. Every country has a soul. Why do we need soul marketing?

A person, an organization, everyone, and everything have a soul, mind, and body. Soul is the boss. If the soul of a person or the soul of an organization hears and loves what you have to market, the mind and body of the person or the organization will follow. Soul marketing is a spiritual treasure for you and humanity.

Soul marketing is to market to the souls of your clients and the souls of the groups and organizations affiliated with your business. If your business is related to all of humanity, you absolutely can soul market your business to every human being!

The significance and benefits of soul marketing can be summarized in one sentence:

**Market to the souls of your business' current and potential
clients and affiliates first; then success of physical marketing to
clients and affiliates and success of your business will follow.**

As an example, let me show you how I do soul marketing for this book. I always use the Four Power Techniques:

Body Power. I sit up straight. I put my left palm over my Message Center and my right hand in the traditional prayer position. See figure 1 on page 61. You learned and applied this Soul Light Era Universal Service Hand Position for Body Power in the practice in chapter six. It is a special hand position for soul-to-soul communication in the Soul Light Era, the new universal era that began in 2003.

When you use this hand position, the Divine, buddhas, holy saints, Taoist saints, angels, archangels, ascended masters, gurus, lamas, and all kinds of spiritual fathers and mothers pay attention to you right away.

Soul Power. I say *hello*:

> *Dear soul mind body of all 7.4 billion souls of humanity,*
> *Dear soul mind body of every country, every city, every organization, every media, every website,*
> *Dear soul mind body of every bookseller, including those online,*
> *Dear soul mind body of publishers of books in every format,*
> *I love you, honor you, and appreciate you.*
> *I am delighted to announce to all of you that the book* Soul Over Matter: Ancient and Modern Wisdom and Practical Techniques to Create Unlimited Abundance, *will be available to humanity on July 12, 2016.*
> *There are many good books that teach about financial abundance.*
> *There are many great teachers who teach about financial abundance in all kinds of workshops, seminars, retreats, and training programs.*
> Soul Over Matter *teaches divine financial abundance. It shares divine and Tao secrets, wisdom, knowledge, and practical techniques to transform finances and business. The root cause of failure in every aspect of life is bad karma. This book teaches you how to self-clear your bad karma in order to transform your finances and business.*
> *Dear Tao Rainbow Light Ball and Rainbow Liquid Spring of Tao Love Soul Mind Body Transplants,*
> *Dear Tao Rainbow Light Ball and Rainbow Liquid Spring of Tao Forgiveness Soul Mind Body Transplants,*
> *Dear Divine,*
> *Dear Tao,*
> *Dear countless healing angels, archangels, ascended masters, buddhas, bodhisattvas, holy saints, Taoist saints, all kinds of saints, all kinds of spiritual fathers and mothers on Mother Earth and in all layers of Heaven,*
> *Dear countless planets, stars, galaxies, and universes,*

I love you, honor you, and appreciate you.
Please bless the book Soul Over Matter.
Spread this book worldwide and allow this book to be a divine
    servant for humanity, Mother Earth, and all universes.
I am very grateful.
Thank you.

Mind Power. I visualize Tao love and forgiveness radiating everywhere to spread the book *Soul Over Matter* worldwide to as many people as possible.

Sound Power. I chant repeatedly for a few minutes, silently or aloud:

Spread the book Soul Over Matter.
Serve humanity and all souls on Mother Earth and in all universes
    for their life transformation.
Spread the book Soul Over Matter.
Serve humanity and all souls on Mother Earth and in all universes
    for their life transformation.
Spread the book Soul Over Matter.
Serve humanity and all souls on Mother Earth and in all universes
    for their life transformation.
Spread the book Soul Over Matter.
Serve humanity and all souls on Mother Earth and in all universes
    for their life transformation. . . .

Close. After chanting for a few minutes, I close:

Hao! Hao! Hao!
Thank you. Thank you. Thank you.

When you do soul marketing, chant for a few minutes per time and do it a few times per day. The more often and the longer you chant, the better.

You can see from the example I just gave you that there are certain basic principles to follow for any soul marketing that you would do for your business or service:

- Use the Four Power Techniques.
  - Body Power — special hand and body positions
  - Soul Power — say *hello* to the souls of your customers and potential customers of your services or business, as well as to current and potential affiliates
  - Mind Power — creative visualization
  - Sound Power — chant sacred mantras, Divine Soul Songs, and more
- Be clear about what you want. Tell the souls straightforwardly about what you are marketing and how you want them to respond. Guide the souls you have called as to what you would like them to do to support you. Be specific, just as though you were in a physical meeting.
- Be sure to tell the souls clearly, sincerely, and honestly that you are offering good service and explain how you are serving. Never do soul marketing for personal gain. This is a *very* important principle. If your intent is selfish, you will not get good results from soul marketing. Your situation could actually become worse because great light beings will not support selfishness. You must be sincere and honest.
- Sincere communication with the souls includes respect, honor, and appreciation for them.
- Spiritual courtesy is very important. Always remember to give gratitude to all of the souls to whom you are soul marketing.
- You must have a powerful opening and closing. There must be a call to action.
- Target important issues when doing soul marketing. Do not ask for trivial things.

Soul marketing has one other important benefit: it saves a lot of money! You do not need to spend physical money to do soul marketing. You can do soul marketing anytime, anywhere.

How to Do Soul Marketing

Here is a simple outline that you can use for soul marketing.

Say *hello*:

Dear _____ (name the souls you wish to market to),

For example, if you are selling shoes, you can say:

Dear every person in my city, every person in my country, all
    humanity,
I love you, honor you, and appreciate you.
Can you come for a short time?
Thank you for coming.
The name of my business is _____.
We produce shoes.

Introduce your shoes and explain how they can benefit the souls you are calling. Tell them where they can find your shoes, and more.
Then chant:

Da Ai, greatest love
Da Ai, greatest love
Da Ai, greatest love
Da Ai, greatest love . . .

Chant for three to five minutes. Then say, "Thank you for coming."
Here is another simple example to promote a book. Say *hello*:

Dear all humanity, please come.
Thank you for coming.

Introduce yourself and your book:

My name is _____.
My book is _____.

Introduce the essence of your book and state clearly how it can benefit the lives of the human beings and souls you have called.

Make sure to speak clearly and to the point. Souls do not like long, repetitive, or useless sentences. Souls are sensitive and do not want to waste time.

Now chant:

> *Da Ai, greatest love*
> *Da Ai, greatest love*
> *Da Ai, greatest love*
> *Da Ai, greatest love . . .*

Chant for three to five minutes.
Close by saying:

> *Thank you so much for listening.*
> *I hope the book transforms your life.*
> *Thank you. Thank you. Thank you.*

Then you can ask the souls you called to return: *Gong Song. Gong Song. Gong Song.* Pronounced *gōng sōng*, this means, "With respect, please return to your abode."

Follow the principles I have explained in this chapter. You can be flexible and creative.

I wish soul marketing would bring abundance and success to your finances and business.

Love you. Love you. Love you.

Thank you. Thank you. Thank you.

Remember all of the principles I have shared.

Remember that what you do, what you speak, and what you think should be to make others happier and healthier and to create love, peace, and harmony for humanity, Mother Earth, and all universes.

Remember never to do soul marketing for selfish reasons, such as for personal gain.

In the physical world, normal marketing for your business could gain you more clients, more friends, and more business associates. In the spiritual world, soul marketing for your business will bring you more soul friends and blessings from the Soul World beyond your comprehension and imagination.

After you read the next chapter, use the ten sacred "Da" qualities as the greatest tools in soul marketing. Apply the ten Da qualities to the souls to whom you market. You could receive better results than from normal soul marketing.

Soul marketing is the new marketing that the vast majority of humanity does not yet know.

Soul marketing is new sacred teaching for the Soul Light Era. It will spread incredibly quickly.

Learn it.

Try it.

Practice it.

Experience it.

Benefit from it.

You will appreciate it.

You will love it.

I wish you great success in your business and finances.

Offer Unconditional Service to Receive Divine Blessings for Success in Finances and Business

People need to make money in business. Money is energy. If one has money and uses it properly, one can gain great virtue. For example, many businesses (and individuals) donate money to support hospitals and schools, to alleviate hunger and poverty, to provide shelter and care for the homeless, to give relief to people struck by disasters, and more. As I explained in chapter four, if you are wealthy, the root cause is good karma: you have offered very good service in previous lifetimes and in this lifetime. Do not forget to continue to serve. Do not forget to share your abundance and blessings.

Many successful businesspeople understand that the more you serve, the more the Divine and Heaven return to you. When I lived in the Philippines, I met a very wealthy person who donated huge amounts of money to build hospitals, schools, and more. He shared with me his realization that after he had donated one million dollars several years prior, he received a few million dollars more the following year. When he donated a few million dollars, he would receive many millions more in the next one or two years. He understood that this was the Divine's and Heaven's continued blessing and reward for his good service.

Remember my teaching: Heaven records everything you do. This is to remind every wealthy person to continue to offer as much good service as you can. This is also to remind every poor person that service is the key to transforming your finances and business.

Serve a little, receive a little blessing.

Serve more, receive more blessings.

Serve unconditionally, receive unlimited blessings.

If you understand this spiritual wisdom, you will know to serve, and to serve more and more.

Serve unconditionally in this lifetime and all of your lifetimes.

8

Applying Soul Over Matter: Ten Practices to Clear Jing Qi Shen Blockages and Manifest Financial Abundance

YOU HAVE LEARNED that the root cause for financial abundance is one's good personal karma and good ancestral karma. I (Master Sha) emphasize again:

Good karma brings financial abundance.
Negative karma blocks financial abundance.

The wisdom of jing qi shen that I shared in previous chapters explains how you can create or block financial abundance.

Shen is the top boss. Shen blockages are soul, heart, and mind blockages. Soul blockages are negative karma, which is the root cause for lack of financial abundance and business success. Heart blockages include impurities such as selfishness, *tan* (greed), *chen* (anger), *chi* (lack of wisdom in speech, behavior, action, and thought), and more. Mind blockages include negative mind-sets, negative attitudes, negative beliefs, ego, attachments, and more.

Qi blockages are blockages in the functions of every aspect of finances and business.

Jing blockages are blockages in the infrastructure of finances and business.

For finances and business to flourish, you need to remove the jing qi shen blockages. The practices in this book are designed to help you remove jing qi shen blockages in your finances and business. Do them, and your finances and business could start to flourish. The more you practice, the more your finances and business could improve.

All of the practices are soul over matter. In one sentence:

Soul over matter can bring great financial and business abundance.

I would like to share the highest spiritual wisdom with you:

The key to creating financial abundance is to serve humanity.

I emphasize again that to serve is to make others happier and healthier. If your business does not have the true purpose to serve humanity and Mother Earth, your financial abundance will be limited. Always remember this most important one-sentence principle to follow for financial abundance:

Serving humanity and Mother Earth by making them happier and healthier can bring unlimited abundance.

Remember the following wisdom that I shared in chapter four:

Soul moves, heart moves.
Heart moves, consciousness moves.
Consciousness moves, energy moves.
Energy moves, matter moves.

These four sacred phrases tell us that if you:

- transform the soul of your finances and business first, then transformation of the heart will follow
- transform the heart of your finances and business, then transformation of the mind (consciousness) will follow
- transform the consciousness of your finances and business, then transformation of the qi, which includes all of the functions in every aspect of business, will follow
- transform the qi of your finances and business, then transformation of the jing, the infrastructure, will follow, bringing success and abundance

This is the sacred wisdom of soul over matter. It is the highest sacred wisdom that has guided every aspect of life in history, including finances and business. I am revealing these secrets in this book to help you achieve financial and business abundance.

Ten Sacred "Da" Qualities

This chapter focuses on practical techniques to remove jing qi shen blockages. There are ten sacred "Da" qualities. "Da" means *greatest* or *highest*. Each quality carries great wisdom to transform your finances and business. I will give you practical techniques for applying the ten Da qualities to bring you financial abundance and business success. The ten Da qualities are the spiritual keys to transforming every aspect of life. They are:

1. Da Ai — *Greatest Love* (pronounced *dah eye*)
2. Da Kuan Shu — *Greatest Forgiveness* (pronounced *dah kwahn shoo*)
3. Da Ci Bei — *Greatest Compassion* (pronounced *dah sz bay*)
4. Da Guang Ming — *Greatest Light* (pronounced *dah gwahng ming*)
5. Da Qian Bei — *Greatest Humility* (pronounced *dah chyen bay*)
6. Da He Xie — *Greatest Harmony* (pronounced *dah huh shyeh*)
7. Da Chang Sheng — *Greatest Flourishing* (pronounced *dah chahng shung*)
8. Da Gan En — *Greatest Gratitude* (pronounced *dah gahn un*)
9. Da Fu Wu — *Greatest Service* (pronounced *dah foo woo*)

10. Da Yuan Man — *Greatest Enlightenment* (pronounced *dah ywen mahn*)

We will apply Five Power Techniques to transform finances and business. These techniques are:

1. **Body Power.** Apply special hand and body positions for spiritual practice to transform finances and business. The one-sentence secret of Body Power is:

    Where you put your hands is where you receive blessings.

2. **Soul Power.** Say *hello* to inner souls (the souls of your systems, organs, parts of the body, cells, DNA, RNA, mind, and more, plus the souls of your finances and business, because you are one team with them) and outer souls (the souls of saints, angels, spiritual fathers and mothers, the Divine, Tao, Mother Earth, and more) to transform finances and business. The one-sentence secret of Soul Power is:

    What you ask of Heaven, Tao (Source), and your own soul is what blessings you will receive.

3. **Mind Power.** Creative visualization to transform finances and business. The one-sentence secret of Mind Power is:

    Where you focus your mind is where you receive blessings.

4. **Sound Power.** Chant sacred mantras to transform finances and business. Mantras are sacred healing sounds and messages that carry Heaven's frequency and vibration to transform finances and business. The one-sentence secret of Sound Power is:

    What you chant is what you become.

5. **Tao Calligraphy Tracing Power.** Tao Calligraphy Tracing Power is using your fingers to trace a Tao (Source) Calligraphy. Tao (Source) Calligraphies are unique modern Chinese calligraphies for healing, blessing, and transforming all life. I introduced Tao Calligraphies to humanity in 2013 in my book *Soul Healing Miracles*.[9] Each Tao Calligraphy I create carries Source jing qi shen that can remove jing qi shen blockages from your finances and business. This book includes two Tao (Source) Calligraphies (figures 3 and 4 in this chapter). The one-sentence secret of Tracing Power is:

Trace Tao Calligraphies to connect with Tao jing qi shen to transform the jing qi shen of your finances and business as well as of every aspect of life.

How Much Do I Need to Do Soul Over Matter Practices?

In this chapter, I give you ten Soul Over Matter practices—one for each of the ten Da qualities. Each practice requires approximately seven minutes. To do all ten Da practices together, the total practice time would be seventy minutes, but you can choose to do as few as two Da practices per day, for a minimum daily practice lasting fourteen minutes. If you really want to transform your finances and business, practice more. There is no shortcut. Devote thirty minutes a day to your Soul Over Matter practice and you could achieve results much faster. Soul Over Matter is sacred wisdom and practice to transform your finances and business in order to bring unlimited abundance.

Remember the guidance. There is no time limit. The more you meditate, the more you chant, and the more you trace the calligraphies, the more benefits you could receive for the flourishing of your finances and business.

I often say:

---

[9] *Soul Healing Miracles: Ancient and New Sacred Wisdom, Knowledge, and Practical Techniques for Healing the Spiritual, Mental, Emotional, and Physical Bodies.* Dallas/Toronto: BenBella Books/ Heaven's Library, 2013.

If you want to know if a pear is sweet, taste it.
If you want to know the power of the ten Da practices, experience it.

The methods I share in this book are extremely simple. They could be too simple to believe. Do the practices anyway. You will experience the power and the benefits.

Soul Over Matter Practices

Let us practice now by applying the Five Power Techniques.

Practice 1. Da Ai (*Greatest Love*)

Body Power. Sit up straight. Put one palm below your navel. Put the other palm over your heart. The lower abdomen is the source for energy, stamina, vitality, and immunity. The heart is the source for greatest love. The heart houses the mind and soul.

Soul Power. Soul Power is to say *hello* to inner souls and outer souls.
  Say *hello* to inner souls:

> *Dear jing qi shen of myself,*
> *Dear jing qi shen of my finances and business* (name your business
>   if you have one),
> *I love you, honor you, and appreciate you.*
> *You have the power to remove jing qi shen blockages of my finances*
>   *and business.*
> *Do a great job!*
> *Thank you.*

  Say *hello* to outer souls:

> *Dear Source,*
> *Dear Heaven and Mother Earth,*
> *Dear saints in Heaven and on Mother Earth,*
> *Dear Tao Calligraphy Da Ai, greatest love,*
> *I love you, honor you, and appreciate you.*

Please bless my finances and business (name your business if you
   have one).
I am extremely grateful.
Thank you.

Mind Power. Visualize light shining in and around your heart.

Sound Power. Chant silently or aloud:

> *Da Ai* (pronounced *dah eye*)
> *Da Ai*
> *Da Ai*
> *Da Ai . . .*

Love melts all blockages and transforms all life. As you chant the
sacred mantra *Da Ai*, close your eyes. Visualize the greatest love from
Heaven and Source, from Heaven's saints, and from your own jing qi
shen shining in your heart.

Yong xin yong nian. "Yong" means *use*. "Xin" means *heart*. "Yong nian"
means *chant*. "Yong xin yong nian" (pronounced *yōng sheen yōng nyen*)
means *use the heart to chant*. This ancient pearl of wisdom teaches us to
chant with our hearts and from our hearts. Using the heart to chant is
ten times more powerful than not using the heart to chant. What does
using the heart to chant mean? To use the heart to chant is to chant very
sincerely and very calmly, with focus and great feeling. It is to *become*
what you chant. Apply this ancient sacred wisdom to use the heart to
chant. You will transform your finances, business, and every aspect of
life faster.

Chant the sacred phrase for seven minutes. At the same time, visualize light shining in your heart. Your finances and business are in your
heart. To chant *Da Ai* while visualizing light in your heart is to visualize
your finances and business shining. Why do you visualize light? There
is another ancient sacred wisdom and practice:

Light shines, all blockages are removed.

Light is one of the most powerful spiritual healings from Heaven and the Source. You can visualize golden or rainbow light during any meditation or chanting.

There is no time limit to chanting *Da Ai* or any of the ten Da qualities. Some Soul Over Matter practitioners who chant for two hours or more per day to self-heal chronic and life-threatening conditions have achieved phenomenal results. Chanting the sacred ten Da mantras to remove jing qi shen blockages for finances and business is beyond powerful. I wish you and every reader would chant longer than seven minutes. The more you chant, the more benefits you could receive.

Tao Calligraphy Tracing Power. Put your five fingertips together to trace the *Da Ai* calligraphy. See figure 2. Each finger connects with a major energy meridian in the body. The Tao (Source) Calligraphy *Da Ai* (see figure 3) carries Source jing qi shen. When you use your fingers to trace the calligraphy, Source jing qi shen can remove the jing qi shen blockages of your finances and business. The Tao Calligraphy carries the purest love and light to purify the jing qi shen of your finances and business.

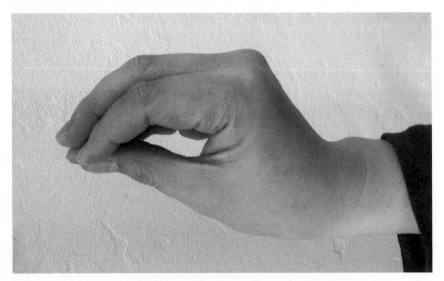

Figure 2. Hand Position for Tao Calligraphy Tracing Power

Before tracing the calligraphy, silently say *hello*:

Dear Tao Source Calligraphy Da Ai,

My name is _____.

I am extremely grateful to ask your Tao Source jing qi shen to remove the jing qi shen blockages of my finances and business.

Thank you.

Then trace the calligraphy for seven minutes as you chant *Da Ai*. Use your heart to chant. Use your heart to trace.

At the end of every practice, always remember to show your gratitude:

Hao! Hao! Hao!

Thank you. Thank you. Thank you.

Wisdom of Da Ai

"Da" means *greatest*. "Ai" means love. "Da Ai" means *greatest love*. Love melts all blockages and transforms all life. Every human being needs love. When you feel love from your parents, when you feel love from your colleagues, when you feel love from your partner, when you feel love from your children, when you feel love from your spiritual fathers or mothers, you are moved and touched. Da Ai is the number one principle to transform finances and business. If everyone in a company could apply love toward each other, transformation of the company's finances could be beyond comprehension.

Learn and do the Soul Over Matter practice of Da Ai. When you are ready, share the practice with your colleagues and employees. You could also share the practice with your family and friends. Da Ai is not only to transform your finances and business; it is the greatest healer to heal all kinds of sickness, including sickness in the physical body, emotional body, mental body, and spiritual body. Da Ai can transform all kinds of relationships. Da Ai can open one's heart and soul. Da Ai can increase wisdom and intelligence. Da Ai can open one's spiritual channels. Da Ai can transform all life.

In this book, we focus on transforming finances and business, but understand that the wisdom and Soul Over Matter practices of the ten Da qualities are the nature of Heaven and Source. The ten Da qualities will serve you in every aspect of life, including health, relationships, finances, intelligence, and spiritual journey, and bring success in every aspect of life.

Four sacred phrases share key wisdom of Da Ai:

一施大愛

Yi Shi Da Ai

無條件愛

Wu Tiao Jian Ai

融化災難

Rong Hua Zai Nan

心清神明

Xin Qing Shen Ming

Yi Shi Da Ai. "Yi" means *one* or *first*. "Shi" means *give*. "Da" means *greatest*. "Ai" means *love*. "Yi shi da ai" (pronounced *ee shr dah eye*) means *the first of the ten Da qualities is greatest love.*

Wu Tiao Jian Ai. "Wu" means *no*. "Tiao jian" means *condition*. "Wu tiao jian ai" (pronounced *woo tee-yow jyen eye*) means *give unconditional love to others*. Think about it. The sun, the moon, the stars, Mother Earth, and Heaven are giving unconditional love in every moment. Tao is the Creator. Tao creates Heaven, Mother Earth, human beings, and countless planets, stars, galaxies, and universes. In every moment, Tao is giving unconditional love. Unconditional love *is* Tao love and Heaven's love. Give unconditional love and you could receive unlimited blessings for health, relationships, financial abundance, and business success.

Rong Hua Zai Nan. "Rong hua" means *melt*. "Zai nan" means *disasters*. "Rong hua zai nan" (pronounced *rōng hwah dzye nahn*) means *melt all disasters and challenges*. This sentence teaches us the benefits of offering unconditional love. Unconditional love is easy to say, but difficult to achieve. We need to offer more and more love. Always hold this wisdom in your heart and soul. In one sentence:

**The more unconditional love you can give to others,
the more financial abundance and success in business
and in every aspect of life can be achieved.**

Xin Qing Shen Ming. "Xin" means *heart*. "Qing" means *clear* or *transparent*. "Shen" means *soul*. "Ming" means *enlighten*. "Xin qing shen ming" (pronounced *sheen ching shun ming*) means *heart is clear and transparent and soul is enlightened*. Enlightenment means your soul has reached the level of a saint or a buddha.

The wisdom of Da Ai in these four sacred phrases can be expressed as follows:
Yi Shi Da Ai. *The first of the ten Da Soul Over Matter practices is to give greatest love to Heaven, Mother Earth, humanity, animals, nature, and countless planets, stars, galaxies, and universes.*
Wu Tiao Jian Ai. *Give this love unconditionally.*
Rong Hua Zai Nan. *The greatest love, which is unconditional love, can remove all kinds of disasters and challenges.*
Xin Qing Shen Ming. *If you offer Da Ai, your heart will be clear and transparent, and your soul will be enlightened.*

Practice 2. Da Kuan Shu (*Greatest Forgiveness*)

"Kuan shu" means *forgiveness*. "Da Kuan Shu" (pronounced *dah kwahn shoo*) means *greatest forgiveness*. Forgiveness is the key to bring love, peace, and harmony.

Wisdom of Da Kuan Shu

Within a family or a business there could be many conflicts and challenges. Applying forgiveness is vital to transform these blockages. To flourish financially it is vital to have love, peace, and harmony. Ancient wisdom is that love, peace, and harmony can bring great financial abundance. Without forgiveness, true love, peace, and harmony cannot be achieved.

Forgiveness practice is the key to self-clear one's negative personal and ancestral karma. The one-sentence secret about karma that I shared in my book *The Power of Soul* is:

Karma is the root cause of success and failure in every aspect of life.

Doing forgiveness practice could clear your root blockages in finances and business.

In fact, doing forgiveness practice sincerely is vital to achieve financial abundance. The more you do forgiveness practice, the more flourishing you could achieve. Some people may think that they already have great financial flourishing without doing this kind of practice. Remember the teaching that these individuals have good karma from their previous and present lifetimes. Good karma brings a lot of virtue, which is Heaven's flowers. This good virtue, along with their and their business team's effort, has brought financial abundance. Even so, forgiveness practice could make their finances and business flourish even more. No one can say that they have never made any mistakes. Everyone makes mistakes in every lifetime. Everyone needs forgiveness. In one sentence:

Forgiveness practice is the golden pearl to transform your finances and business.

Four sacred phrases share key wisdom of Da Kuan Shu:

二大寬恕
Er Da Kuan Shu

我原諒你
Wo Yuan Liang Ni

你原諒我
Ni Yuan Liang Wo

相愛平安和諧
Xiang Ai Ping An He Xie

Er Da Kuan Shu. "Er" means *two* or *second*. "Da" means *greatest*. "Kuan shu" means *forgiveness*. "Er da kuan shu" (pronounced *ur dah kwahn shoo*) means *the second of the ten Da qualities is greatest forgiveness*.

Wo Yuan Liang Ni. "Wo" means *I*. "Yuan liang" means *forgive*. "Ni" means *you*. "Wo yuan liang ni" (pronounced *waw ywen lyahng nee*) means *I forgive you*. Two or more people could have many challenges in their relationships with each other. To apply true forgiveness is a priceless treasure to bring love, peace, and harmony to relationships, organizations, and businesses. First you need to forgive others for all of the mistakes they have made in this lifetime and in past lifetimes to hurt or harm you. This is true forgiveness. Some people cannot forgive. If one cannot forgive, one will continue to suffer.

Ni Yuan Liang Wo. "Ni yuan liang wo" (pronounced *nee ywen lyahng waw*) means *you forgive me*. Chant this phrase and ask everyone that you have hurt or harmed in any lifetime to forgive you. Sincerely request their forgiveness.

Xiang Ai Ping An He Xie. "Xiang ai" means *love*. "Ping an" means *peace*. "He xie" means *harmony*. "Xiang ai ping an he xie" (pronounced *shyahng eye ping ahn huh shyeh*) means *love, peace, and harmony*.

In summary, these four sacred phrases can be expressed as follows:

Er Da Kuan Shu. *The second of the ten Da Soul Over Matter practices is to develop greatest forgiveness.*

Wo Yuan Liang Ni. *I forgive you.*

Ni Yuan Liang Wo. *You forgive me.*

Xiang Ai Ping An He Xie. *Bring love, peace, and harmony.*

I cannot emphasize enough the importance of doing regular forgiveness practice.

Let us do the Soul Over Matter practice of Da Kuan Shu now. Apply the Five Power Techniques:

Body Power. Place one palm below your navel. Place the other palm over your heart. Forgiveness comes from your heart and soul.

Soul Power. Say *hello* and do a sincere forgiveness practice:

> *Dear all jing qi shen of every human being and every business that my ancestors, I, and our businesses have hurt or harmed in this lifetime and in previous lifetimes,*
> *We deeply apologize.*
> *Please forgive us.*
> *We know in our hearts that only to ask for forgiveness is not enough.*
> *We have to serve.*
> *To serve is to make others happier and healthier.*
> *We will offer more humanitarian service.*
> *We will chant and meditate more.*
> *We will serve unconditionally.*
> *Thank you so much.*

> *Dear everyone and everything that has hurt or harmed my ancestors, our businesses, and me in all lifetimes,*
> *I totally forgive you. I forgive you unconditionally.*

Say *hello* to outer souls:

> *Dear Source,*
> *Dear Heaven and Mother Earth,*
> *Dear all saints in Heaven and on Mother Earth,*
> *Dear Tao Source Calligraphy Da Kuan Shu,*
> *Please forgive my ancestors, me, and our businesses for all of the mistakes we have made related to finances and business or in any other aspect of life through our many lifetimes.*
> *I am extremely honored and grateful.*
> *I know in my heart that only to ask for forgiveness is not enough.*
> *I have to serve.*
> *Serve. Serve. Serve.*
> *I cannot serve enough.*
> *Thank you.*

Mind Power. Visualize golden light shining in and around your heart.

Sound Power. Chant silently or aloud:

> *Da Kuan Shu* (pronounced *dah kwahn shoo*)
> *Da Kuan Shu*
> *Da Kuan Shu*
> *Da Kuan Shu* . . .

Tao Calligraphy Tracing Power. Put your five fingertips together to trace the Tao Source Calligraphy *Da Kuan Shu*. See figure 4. The Tao (Source) Calligraphy *Da Kuan Shu* carries Source jing qi shen. When you trace the calligraphy, Source jing qi shen can remove jing qi shen blockages from your finances and business.

Before tracing the calligraphy, silently say *hello*:

> *Dear Tao Source Calligraphy* Da Kuan Shu,
> *My name is* _____.
> *I am extremely grateful to ask your Tao Source jing qi shen to remove the jing qi shen blockages of my finances and business.*
> *Thank you.*

Then trace the calligraphy for seven minutes or more as you chant *Da Kuan Shu*. Use your heart to chant. Use your heart to trace.

Close the practice:

> *Hao! Hao! Hao!*
> *Thank you. Thank you. Thank you.*

Forgiveness practice is a key to remove negative karma. To remove negative karma is to remove the root cause of blockages in finances, business, and every aspect of life. Therefore, I suggest that you chant for at least fifteen minutes. There is no upper limit. You could chant for a half hour or an hour. The benefits could be beyond comprehension.

If you have challenges with anyone, you can do the following forgiveness practice on a soul level, without being face-to-face with the person.

Dear soul mind body of _____ (name the person),
Please come.
I would like to do a forgiveness practice with you.
I deeply apologize for all of the mistakes and harm my ancestors and
    I have done to you in this lifetime and past lifetimes.
I ask you to forgive my ancestors and me.
For any harm that you and your ancestors have done to my
    ancestors and me, we totally forgive you and your ancestors.
Let us chant together, heart to heart, soul to soul.
Thank you.

Then chant:

I forgive you.
You forgive me.
Bring love, peace, and harmony.
Bring love, peace, and harmony.

I forgive you.
You forgive me.
Bring love, peace, and harmony.
Bring love, peace, and harmony.

I forgive you.
You forgive me.
Bring love, peace, and harmony.
Bring love, peace, and harmony.

I forgive you.
You forgive me.
Bring love, peace, and harmony.
Bring love, peace, and harmony. . . .

Chant for seven minutes or more. Then close the practice:

Hao! Hao! Hao!
Thank you. Thank you. Thank you.

Forgiveness practice is not a one-time practice. It is a daily practice. Forgiveness practice transforms all life, including finances and business. The Soul Over Matter practices of the ten Da qualities are so simple, but they are very powerful. The reason is that the ten Da qualities are the nature of Heaven and Source. They carry the purest love and light with Heaven's and Tao jing qi shen, which can purify the jing qi shen of our finances, business, and every aspect of life.

I share a powerful ancient wisdom: *If a fish lives in polluted water, the fish either becomes sick or dies.* To save the fish, we must cleanse and purify the water. Our health and our finances have all kinds of jing qi shen blockages. Jing qi shen blockages are pollution. We need to purify this internal pollution. The ten Da qualities have the power to clear all kinds of jing qi shen blockages in every aspect of life, bringing good health, financial abundance, and success.

Practice 3. Da Ci Bei (*Greatest Compassion*)

"Ci bei" means *compassion*. "Da Ci Bei" (pronounced *dah sz bay*) means *greatest compassion*. Compassion boosts energy, stamina, vitality, and immunity.

Four sacred phrases share key wisdom of Da Ci Bei:

三大慈悲
San Da Ci Bei

願力增強
Yuan Li Zeng Qiang

服務眾生
Fu Wu Zhong Sheng
功德無量
Gong De Wu Liang

San Da Ci Bei. "San" means *three* or *third*. "Da ci bei" means *greatest compassion.* "San da ci bei" (pronounced *sahn dah sz bay*) means *the third of the ten Da qualities is greatest compassion.*

Yuan Li Zeng Qiang. "Yuan" means *will.* "Li" means *strength.* "Zeng qiang" means *increase.* "Yuan li zeng qiang" (pronounced *ywen lee dzung chyahng*) means *increase willpower.* In ancient wisdom, compassion increases willpower. Compassion carries strength to transform finances and business.

Fu Wu Zhong Sheng. "Fu wu" means *service.* "Zhong sheng" means *humanity.* "Fu wu zhong sheng" (pronounced *foo woo jōng shung*) means *serve humanity.*

Gong De Wu Liang. "Gong de" means *virtue.* "Wu liang" means *immeasurable.* "Gong de wu liang" (pronounced *gōng duh woo lyahng*) means *immeasurable virtue.*

These four sacred phrases can be summarized as follows:
San Da Ci Bei. *The third of the ten Da sacred Soul Over Matter practices is greatest compassion.*
Yuan Li Zeng Qiang. *Increase willpower.*
Fu Wu Zhong Sheng. *Serve humanity.*
Gong De Wu Liang. *The virtue will be immeasurable.*
On Mother Earth, a person works for a company. At the end of the month, he or she receives a salary. Salary is the company's appreciation for the employee's work. In the spiritual realm, when a person offers love, care, and compassion to others, Heaven will give the person virtue, which is Heaven's appreciation and flowers. Heaven's flowers are deposited in the person's virtue bank account in Heaven. This spiritual currency can transform to physical financial abundance on Mother Earth.
Greatest compassion (Da Ci Bei) boosts energy, stamina, vitality, immunity, and willpower. These are vital for financial and business abundance.
Let us do a Soul Over Matter practice now to apply Da Ci Bei to bless your finances and business. Use the Four Power Techniques:

Body Power. Place one palm below your navel. Place the other palm over your heart.

Soul Power. Say *hello* to inner souls:

Dear soul mind body of myself,
Dear soul mind body of all my financial and business team members
    and leaders on Mother Earth,
I love you, honor you, and appreciate you.
Let us practice compassion to increase our willpower and boost our
    energy, stamina, vitality, and immunity.
Do a great job!
Thank you.

Say *hello* to outer souls:

Dear Source,
Dear Heaven and Mother Earth,
Dear all saints in Heaven and on Mother Earth,
Dear Da Ci Bei, greatest compassion,
Please bless me and my whole team in finances and business
    so that we can serve more and more.
The more we serve, the more virtue Heaven will give to us.
The more flourishing could come to our finances and business.
We are extremely grateful.
Thank you.

Mind Power. Focus your mind on the heart area and visualize golden light shining in your finances and business.

Sound Power. Chant aloud or silently:

Da Ci Bei (pronounced *dah sz bay*)
Da Ci Bei
Da Ci Bei
Da Ci Bei . . .

Chant for at least seven minutes. Use your heart to chant. The more you chant, the better.

Close the practice in the usual way:

Hao! Hao! Hao!
Thank you. Thank you. Thank you.

Practice 4. Da Guang Ming (*Greatest Light*)

"Guang" means *light.* "Ming" means *transparency.* "Da Guang Ming" (pronounced *dah gwahng ming*) means *greatest light and transparency.*

Four sacred phrases share key wisdom of Da Guang Ming:

四大光明

Si Da Guang Ming

我在道光中

Wo Zai Tao Guang Zhong

道光在我中

Tao Guang Zai Wo Zhong

通體透明

Tong Ti Tou Ming

Si Da Guang Ming. "Si" means *four* or *fourth.* "Da" means *greatest.* "Guang" means *light.* "Ming" means *transparency.* "Si da guang ming" (pronounced *sz dah gwahng ming*) means *the fourth of the ten Da qualities is greatest light and transparency.*

Wo Zai Tao Guang Zhong. "Wo" means *I.* "Zai" means *be at.* Tao is Source, the Creator. "Guang" means *light.* "Zhong" means *within.* "Wo zai Tao guang zhong" (pronounced *waw dzye dow gwahng jōng*) means *I am within Tao Source light.* This sacred phrase is so vital to nourish your finances, your business, your health, your relationships, and every aspect of your life. Imagine you are within Tao Source light. Tao Source light carries Source jing qi shen, which is the purest jing qi shen with the greatest power to transform the jing qi shen of your finances, business, and every aspect of life. This chanting and visualization are beyond powerful. Practice more. Benefit more.

Tao Guang Zai Wo Zhong. "Tao guang zai wo zhong" (pronounced *dow gwahng dzye waw jōng*) means *Tao Source light is within me*. Imagine Tao Source light inside your body and inside your finances and business. How much blessing could you, your finances, and business receive from Tao Source light? You can chant this and the previous sacred phrase any time and all of the time to bless your finances, your business, and yourself.

Chant silently or aloud:

> *Wo zai Tao guang zhong, Tao guang zai wo zhong.*

or

> *I am inside Tao Source light, Tao Source light is inside me.*

or

> *My finances and business are within Tao Source light,*
> *Tao Source light is within my finances and business.*

Chant more:

> *My finances and business are within Tao Source light,*
> *Tao Source light is within my finances and business.*
> *My finances and business are within Tao Source light,*
> *Tao Source light is within my finances and business.*
> *My finances and business are within Tao Source light,*
> *Tao Source light is within my finances and business.*
> *My finances and business are within Tao Source light,*
> *Tao Source light is within my finances and business. . . .*

Close your eyes and chant for a few more minutes. Focus your mind on your heart.

Tong Ti Tou Ming. "Tong" means *whole*. "Ti" means *body*. "Tou ming" means *transparent*. "Tong ti tou ming" (pronounced *tōng tee tō ming*) means *the whole body is transparent.*

These four sacred phrases can be summarized as follows:

Si Da Guang Ming. *The fourth of the ten Da Soul Over Matter practices is greatest light and transparency.*

Wo Zai Tao Guang Zhong. *I am inside Tao Source light.*

Tao Guang Zai Wo Zhong. *Tao Source light is inside me.*

Tong Ti Tou Ming. *The whole body is transparent.*

Let us do a practice now to apply Da Guang Ming to bless your finances and business. Use the Four Power Techniques:

Body Power. Place one palm below your navel. Place the other palm over your Ming Men area. "Ming" means *life*. "Men" means *gate*. "Ming Men" means *life gate*. The Ming Men area is a sacred place in your lower back, in front of and above the sacrum. In yogic practice, the Ming Men area is known as the kundalini.

Soul Power. Say *hello* to inner souls:

> *Dear soul mind body of myself,*
> *Dear soul mind body of my finances and business* (name your
> > business if you have one),
> *I love you, honor you, and appreciate you.*
> *You have the power to bless my finances and business.*
> *Do a great job!*
> *Thank you.*

Say *hello* to outer souls:

> *Dear Source,*
> *Dear Heaven and Mother Earth,*

Dear all saints in Heaven and on Mother Earth,
Dear Da Guang Ming, greatest light,
Please shine Tao Source light into my finances and business.
I am extremely grateful.
Thank you.

Mind Power. Put your mind on the Ming Men area and visualize golden Tao Source light shining in your finances and business.

Sound Power. Chant silently or aloud:

Da Guang Ming (pronounced *dah gwahng ming*)
Da Guang Ming
Da Guang Ming
Da Guang Ming . . .

Keep chanting:

My finances and business are inside Tao Source light,
   Tao Source light is inside my finances and business.
My finances and business are inside Tao Source light,
   Tao Source light is inside my finances and business.
My finances and business are inside Tao Source light,
   Tao Source light is inside my finances and business.
My finances and business are inside Tao Source light,
   Tao Source light is inside my finances and business. . . .

Chant for at least seven minutes. Use your heart to chant. The more you chant, the better.

Hao! Hao! Hao!
Thank you. Thank you. Thank you.

Practice 5. Da Qian Bei (*Greatest Humility*)

"Qian bei" means *humility*. "Da Qian Bei" (pronounced *dah chyen bay*) means *greatest humility*. In ancient Chinese wisdom, humility is the key for progress. For centuries, young Chinese children have been taught this six-word couplet:

qian shou yi, man zhao sun

"Qian" means *humility*. "Shou" means *receive*. "Yi" means *benefit*. "Man" means *pride*. "Zhao" means *attract*. "Sun" means *reduce* and *harm*. "Qian shou yi, man zhao sun" (pronounced *chyen shō ee, mahn jow swun*) means *humility receives benefits, pride reduces success*. The King James Bible says, a little more strongly, "Pride goeth before destruction, and a haughty spirit before a fall."

Five sacred phrases share key wisdom of Da Qian Bei:

五大謙卑

Wu Da Qian Bei

柔弱不爭

Rou Ruo Bu Zheng

持續精進

Chi Xu Jing Jin

失謙卑

Shi Qian Bei

跌萬丈

Die Wan Zhang

Wu Da Qian Bei. "Wu" means *five* or *fifth*. "Da" means *greatest*. "Qian bei" means *humility*. "Wu da qian bei" (pronounced *woo dah chyen bay*) means *the fifth of the ten Da qualities is greatest humility*.

Rou Ruo Bu Zheng. "Rou" means *soft* or *gentle*. "Ruo" means *weak*. "Bu" means *not*. "Zheng" means *fight, strive,* or *argue*. "Rou ruo bu zheng" (pronounced *rō rwaw boo jung*) means *soft and weak, do not fight, strive, or argue*.

This is a key teaching from the *Dao De Jing*. Lao Zi expressed it as:

rou ruo sheng gang qiang

"Rou ruo" means *soft and weak*. "Sheng" means *overcome*. "Gang qiang" means *strong, firm, unyielding*. "Rou ruo sheng gang qiang" (pronounced *rō rwaw shung gahng chyahng*) means *the soft and weak can overcome the strong*.

There is another famous ancient sacred Chinese phrase:

di shui chuan shi

"Di" means *drop*. "Shui" means *water*. "Chuan" means *go through*. "Shi" means *stone*. "Di shui chuan shi" (pronounced *dee shway chwahn shr*) means *a drop of water can go through stone*. Water is soft and weak. A stone is hard and strong. Yet if drops of water continue to fall on a stone, eventually the water can drill a hole through the stone.

Lao Zi realized that weak and delicate things can have great tenacity. Weak things also can have great hidden inner vitality. They could have huge invisible potential power. On the other hand, strong things may only appear strong or their strength could be very limited. Therefore, strong things could be very vulnerable. "Rou ruo sheng gang qiang" is great wisdom from Lao Zi. Many examples in history have demonstrated this great wisdom.

"Bu zheng" is also a great teaching of Lao Zi. No striving, no fighting, and no arguing is the nature of Tao. Tao creates Heaven, Mother Earth, and countless planets, stars, galaxies, and universes. Tao creates every human being, but does Tao control anyone? No! Everyone has free will. Tao gives everyone freedom to walk his or her own path. Tao does not fight or argue with anyone.

Rou ruo bu zheng (*soft and weak, do not fight, strive, or argue*) is a Tao quality. It may be hard for some to understand, but follow the wisdom and you could receive remarkable benefits for your finances and business, as well as your health, relationships, and every aspect of life.

Chi Xu Jing Jin. "Chi xu" means *persistence*. "Jing jin" means *forge ahead vigorously* or *dedicate oneself to progress*. "Chi xu jing jin" (pronounced *chee shü jing jeen*) means *be persistent and dedicate yourself to progress*.

Shi Qian Bei. "Shi" means *lose*. "Qian bei" means *humility*. "Shi qian bei" (pronounced *shr chyen bay*) means *lose humility*.

Die Wan Zhang. "Die" means *fall down*. "Wan" means *ten thousand*. In Chinese, ten thousand represents *all* or *countless*. "Zhang" is an ancient unit of length, equivalent to nearly eleven feet. "Die wan zhang" (pronounced *dyeh wahn jahng*) expresses *fall down into the deepest cavern*.

These five sacred phrases can be summarized as follows:

Wu Da Qian Bei. *The fifth of the ten Da Soul Over Matter practices is greatest humility.*

Rou Ruo Bu Zheng. *Gentle and weak, do not fight, strive, or argue.*

Chi Xu Jing Jin. *Persistently forge ahead vigorously.*

Shi Qian Bei. *Lose humility.*

Die Wan Zhang. *Fall into the deepest cavern.*

These five sacred phrases teach us that humility is a key for progress in finances, business, and every aspect of life. They teach us that the Tao qualities of softness and weakness can overcome strength and hardness. Striving, fighting, and arguing are not Tao qualities. This wisdom warns us that if we or our business lose humility, we or our business could drop dramatically.

Let us do the Soul Over Matter practice of Da Qian Bei now. Apply the Four Power Techniques:

Body Power. Place one palm below your navel. Place the other palm over your heart.

Soul Power. Say *hello* to inner souls:

Dear soul mind body of myself,

Dear soul mind body of my finances and business (name your
    business if you have one),
I love you, honor you, and appreciate you.
You have the power to remove the jing qi shen blockages of ego and
    pride.
Do a great job!
Thank you.

Say *hello* to outer souls:

Dear Source,
Dear Heaven and Mother Earth,
Dear all saints in Heaven and on Mother Earth,
Dear Da Qian Bei, greatest humility,
Please remove my jing qi shen blockages of ego and pride, especially
    blockages related to my finances and business.
Help me to develop humility.
Help me to follow the Tao principles of soft and weak, no fighting,
    striving, or arguing.
I am extremely grateful.
Thank you.

Mind Power. Gently focus your mind around your heart and visualize
golden light shining in your finances and business.

Sound Power. Chant silently or aloud:

Da Qian Bei (pronounced *dah chyen bay*)
Da Qian Bei
Da Qian Bei
Da Qian Bei . . .

Use your heart to chant. The more you chant, the better. Chant for at
least seven minutes, then close:

Hao! Hao! Hao!

Thank you. Thank you. Thank you.

Practice 6. Da He Xie (*Greatest Harmony*)

"He xie" means *harmony*. "Da He Xie" (pronounced *dah huh shyeh*) means *greatest harmony*.

Four sacred phrases share key wisdom of Da He Xie:

六大和諧

Liu Da He Xie

三人同心

San Ren Tong Xin

齊力斷金

Qi Li Duan Jin

成功秘訣

Cheng Gong Mi Jue

Liu Da He Xie. "Liu" means *six* or *sixth*. "Da" means *greatest*. "He xie" means *harmony*. "Liu da he xie" (pronounced *leo dah huh shyeh*) means *the sixth of the ten Da qualities is greatest harmony*.

San Ren Tong Xin. "San" means *three*. "Ren" means *person*. "Tong" means *similar* or *together*. "Xin" means *heart*. "San ren tong xin" (pronounced *sahn wren tōng sheen*) means *three people join hearts together*.

Qi Li Duan Jin. "Qi" means *together*. "Li" means *strength*. "Duan" means *cut*. "Jin" means *gold*. "Qi li duan jin" (pronounced *chee lee dwahn jeen*) means *combined strength can cut gold*.

San ren tong xin, qi li duan jin is a teaching from the *I Ching*, the renowned ancient Chinese classic that is a treasure to unlock the sacred code of humanity and the universe.

Cheng Gong Mi Jue. "Cheng gong" means *success.* "Mi jue" means *secret.* "Cheng gong mi jue" (pronounced *chung gōng mee jooeh*) means *secret of success.*

These four sacred phrases can be summarized as follows:

Liu Da He Xie. *The sixth of the ten Da Soul Over Matter practices is greatest harmony.*

San Ren Tong Xin. *Three people join their hearts together.*

Qi Li Duan Jin. *Their strength can cut gold.*

Cheng Gong Mi Jue. *The secret of success.*

The sacred message and teaching of these four phrases can be summarized in one sentence:

Harmony of the business team is a key for success.

Let us do a Soul Over Matter practice now to develop Da He Xie. Apply the Four Power Techniques:

Body Power. Place one palm below your navel. Place the other palm over your heart.

Soul Power. Say *hello* to inner souls:

> *Dear soul mind body of myself,*
> *Dear soul mind body of my business team members,*
> *I love you, honor you, and appreciate you.*
> *You have the power to be harmonized.*
> *Do a great job!*
> *Thank you.*

Say *hello* to outer souls:

> *Dear Source,*
> *Dear Heaven and Mother Earth,*
> *Dear all saints in Heaven and on Mother Earth,*
> *Dear Da He Xie, greatest harmony,*

> *Please bless all of my business team members and me with harmony*
>   *in order to have great success.*
> *We are extremely grateful.*
> *Thank you.*

Mind Power. Focus on the heart area and visualize golden light shining in your whole business team.

Sound Power. Chant silently or aloud:

> *Da He Xie* (pronounced *dah huh shyeh*)
> *Da He Xie*
> *Da He Xie*
> *Da He Xie . . .*

Chant for at least seven minutes. Use your heart to chant. The more you chant, the better.

> *Hao! Hao! Hao!*
> *Thank you. Thank you. Thank you.*

The more you do this Soul Over Matter practice, the more harmonized your financial and business team could become. This harmony could bring financial abundance. Remember the wisdom: Soul Over Matter practices work at the soul level, which affects the heart and consciousness. When the soul moves and acts, the functions (qi) and materials (jing) in your finances and business will move, helping you to create financial abundance.

Practice 7. Da Chang Sheng (*Greatest Flourishing*)

"Da" means *greatest*. "Chang sheng" means *flourishing*. "Da Chang Sheng" (pronounced *dah chahng shung*) means *greatest flourishing*.

Four sacred phrases share key wisdom of Da Chang Sheng:

Figure 3. Tao Calligraphy *Da Ai*

Figure 4. Tao Calligraphy *Da Kuan Shu*

七大昌盛
Qi Da Chang Sheng

道賜盈福
Tao Ci Ying Fu

行善積德
Xing Shan Ji De

道業昌盛
Tao Ye Chang Sheng

Qi Da Chang Sheng. "Qi" means *seven* or *seventh*. "Da" means *greatest*. "Chang sheng" means *flourish* or *prosper*. "Qi da chang sheng" (pronounced *chee dah chahng shung*) means *the seventh of the ten Da qualities is greatest flourishing.*

Millions of people on Mother Earth wish for the greatest flourishing in their finances and business. Why do we need good finances? Money is great energy. That energy must be directed in the proper way. What is the proper way? *If we have good finances, we can serve more.*

There is very important ancient wisdom that teaches us the true value and purpose of money. If a person has great wealth but uses the money in improper ways, such as gambling, supporting those who cause harm or take advantage of others, or keeping it to indulge in a life of opulence and luxury, it could create huge negative karma. This person could learn huge lessons by using money in improper ways.

On the other hand, if a person uses money in the proper way, such as serving the poor, serving victims of disasters, and supporting other humanitarian efforts, he or she could receive huge blessings. In one sentence:

The true purpose of money is to serve others better by making others happier and healthier.

Tao Ci Ying Fu. Tao is Source. "Ci" means *bestow.* "Ying" means *huge.* "Fu" means *prosperity, luck, flourishing,* and *success. Fu* is one of the most powerful words in the Chinese language. "Tao ci ying fu" (pronounced *dow sz ying foo*) means *Tao Source bestows huge prosperity and flourishing.*

I shared earlier that the root cause of one's wealth is positive virtue (good karma) that has accumulated through all lifetimes, past and present. Positive virtue is the record of good services, including love, forgiveness, care, compassion, sincerity, honesty, generosity, kindness, purity, integrity, and much more.

According to ancient wisdom, positive virtue determines how much financial flourishing, good health, and good relationships a person enjoys. It even determines how long a person lives as a physical being. If you have great financial flourishing, congratulations! If you do not have enough financial flourishing, remember to remove jing qi shen blockages of your finances and business and serve others unconditionally to accumulate good virtue.

Why am I leading you in this chapter to do Soul Over Matter practices of the ten Da qualities? To do these practices is to bring Tao Source and Heaven's jing qi shen to your finances and business. The frequency and vibration of Tao Source jing qi shen purifies and cleanses the jing qi shen of your finances and business. Doing the ten Da Soul Over Matter practices is a great service in itself. You are chanting. You are meditating. You are tracing Tao Source Calligraphies. As you are bringing Tao Source and Heaven's jing qi shen to your finances and business, you are at the same time bringing Tao Source and Heaven's jing qi shen to humanity and Mother Earth. Doing the ten Da practices is one of the greatest services you can offer. You are serving humanity and Mother Earth. You are bringing them virtue. The virtue you receive can enhance and bring abundance to your finances and business.

I cannot emphasize enough Tao Source Soul Over Matter practices of the ten Da qualities. It could take time to truly understand the depth, significance, and power of these practices. Please start to do them regularly. Do them more and more. Have trust. Practice, practice, practice, and reap the benefits.

Tao is the ultimate Creator and Source. Tao belongs to the Wu World, which is the world of *emptiness* and *nothingness*. The Wu World creates Heaven, Mother Earth, human beings, and countless planets, stars, galaxies, and universes. The Wu World has no limits. We cannot imagine enough the power of the Source. Financial abundance belongs to the You World, which is the world of *existence*. The You (pronounced *yō*) World is always limited. You could be a millionaire, billionaire, or multibillionaire. It does not matter. You have limitations. Everyone and everything on Mother Earth and in countless universes has limitations. Source, the Creator, has no limitations. The Soul Over Matter practices of the ten Da qualities connect directly with Source jing qi shen. The practices can purify and clear the jing qi shen blockages in your finances and business little by little to bring you more and more financial abundance. Remember, you are receiving blessings from Tao Source, which is the Creator. There is no limitation. In one sentence:

The Tao Source Soul Over Matter practices of the ten Da qualities can bring unlimited abundance to your finances and business.

Xing Shan Ji De. "Xing" means *do* or *perform*. "Shan" means *kindness*. Shan includes all kinds of good services such as love, care, compassion, sincerity, honesty, generosity, kindness, grace, integrity, purity, and much more. "Ji" means *accumulate*. "De" means *virtue*. Spiritual law states that when a person offers kind service, Heaven will give virtue (Heaven's flowers) to that person's Akashic Record book. "Xing shan ji de" (pronounced *shing shahn jee duh*) means *offer kind service and accumulate good virtue*.

Good virtue (good karma) is the root cause for financial abundance. The more good virtue one has accumulated in previous lifetimes and in this lifetime, the more financial and business flourishing one will receive.

Tao Ye Chang Sheng. Tao is Source. "Ye" means *career*. "Chang sheng" means *flourish* or *prosper*. "Tao ye chang sheng" (pronounced *dow yuh chahng shung*) means *Tao career flourishes*. This sacred phrase is itself a Tao financial blessing. Please remember this and do Soul Over Matter practices more to create your financial and business abundance.

The above four sacred phrases can be summarized as follows:

Qi Da Chang Sheng. *The seventh of the ten Da Soul Over Matter prac-tices is greatest flourishing.*

Tao Ci Ying Fu. *Tao Source bestows huge prosperity, luck, and success.*

Xing Shan Ji De. *Offer kind service, accumulate good virtue.*

Tao Ye Chang Sheng. *Tao career flourishes.*

Join me now to do a Soul Over Matter practice to help manifest Tao Chang Sheng in your finances, business, and every aspect of life. Apply the Four Power Techniques:

Body Power. Place one palm below your navel. Place the other palm over your heart.

Soul Power. Say *hello* to inner souls:

> *Dear soul mind body of myself,*
> *Dear soul mind body of my finances and business,*
> *I love you, honor you, and appreciate you.*
> *You have the power to prosper and flourish.*
> *Do a great job!*
> *Thank you.*

Say *hello* to outer souls:

> *Dear Source,*
> *Dear Heaven and Mother Earth,*
> *Dear all saints in Heaven and on Mother Earth,*
> *Dear Da Chang Sheng, greatest flourishing,*
> *Please bless all of my finances and business with great prosperity and*
>   *flourishing.*
> *I am extremely grateful.*
> *Thank you.*

Mind Power. Focus your mind on your heart and the area around it. Visualize golden light shining in your finances and business.

Sound Power. Chant silently or aloud:

Da Chang Sheng (pronounced *dah chahng shung*)
Da Chang Sheng
Da Chang Sheng
Da Chang Sheng . . .

Chant for at least seven minutes. Use your heart to chant. As you do the Soul Over Matter practice of Da Chang Sheng, Tao Source is directly blessing your finances and business. Therefore, chant with great sincerity and great respect. You can chant anytime, anywhere. The more you chant, the better. There is no time limit.

Hao! Hao! Hao!
Thank you. Thank you. Thank you.

Practice 8. Da Gan En (*Greatest Gratitude*)

"Gan en" means *gratitude*. "Da Gan En" (pronounced *dah gahn un*) means *greatest gratitude*.
Four sacred phrases share key wisdom of Da Gan En:

八大感恩
Ba Da Gan En

道生德養
Tao Sheng De Yang

栽培賜慧
Zai Pei Ci Hui

道恩永存
Tao En Yong Cun

Ba Da Gan En. "Ba" means *eight* or *eighth*. "Da" means *greatest*. "Gan en" means *gratitude*. *The eighth of the ten Da qualities is greatest gratitude.* Gratitude is a key for further progress. If you receive financial abundance, be sure to show gratitude to Tao Source, to Heaven, to your physical business team, and more. Then you will receive more blessings from Tao Source, Heaven, and your business team. We know in our hearts that gratitude is vital in every aspect of life.

Tao Sheng De Yang. Tao is Source, the ultimate Creator. "Sheng" means *create*. "De" is *the action or expression of Tao Source.* "Yang" means *nourish*. "Tao sheng de yang" (pronounced *dow shung duh yahng*) means *Tao Source creates everyone and everything, including Heaven, Mother Earth, human beings, animals, and countless planets, stars, galaxies, and universes; the action of Tao Source nourishes everyone and everything.* Everyone and everything cannot appreciate Tao Source and *de* enough. It is vital wisdom for a human being to realize the honor and blessing of Tao Source and *de*.

Zai Pei Ci Hui. "Zai pei" means *cultivate*. "Ci" means *bestow*. "Hui" means *wisdom*. "Zai pei ci hui" (pronounced *dzye pay sz hway*) means *Tao cultivates and bestows wisdom and intelligence upon everyone and everything.*

Tao En Yong Cun. Tao is Source. "En" means *favor*. "Yong cun" means *always exist*. "Tao en yong cun" (pronounced *dow un yōng tsoon*) means *the favors and blessings that Tao Source bestows always remain in our hearts and souls.*

These four sacred phrases tell us that Tao Source creates us, nourishes us, raises us, and bestows wisdom and grace upon us to empower us to succeed in every aspect of life. We cannot express enough the greatest gratitude to Tao Source and *de*. Therefore, the honor, favor, grace, and blessings of Tao and *de* should always remain in our hearts and souls.

These four sacred phrases can be summarized as follows:

Ba Da Gan En. *The eighth of the ten Da Soul Over Matter practices is greatest gratitude.*

Tao Sheng De Yang. *Tao Source creates and de, the action and expression of Tao Source, nourishes everyone and everything.*

Zai Pei Ci Hui. *Tao Source cultivates and bestows wisdom and intelligence upon everyone and everything.*

Tao En Yong Cun. *The honor, favor, and grace of Tao Source should remain in our hearts and souls forever.*

Gratitude is very important for your finances and business to prosper and flourish further. In one sentence:

> **Gratitude to Tao Source and Heaven is essential
> in order to receive their further blessings.**

Let us do a Soul Over Matter practice for Da Gan En now. Use the Four Power Techniques:

Body Power. Place one palm below your navel. Place the other palm over your heart.

Soul Power. Say *hello* to inner souls:

> *Dear soul mind body of myself,*
> *Dear soul mind body of all of physical team members related to my*
>   *finances and business,*
> *I love you, honor you, and appreciate you.*
> *You have the power to develop and express more gratitude to Tao*
>   *Source and Heaven, as well as to each other.*
> *Do a great job!*
> *Thank you.*

Say *hello* to outer souls:

> *Dear Source,*
> *Dear Heaven and Mother Earth,*
> *Dear all saints in Heaven and on Mother Earth,*
> *Dear Da Gan En, greatest gratitude,*

We cannot express enough our greatest gratitude to all of you for all
you have given to me and the whole team related to my finances
and business.
Please bless every member of my finance and business teams and me
to have more gratitude in order to receive more success.
We are extremely grateful.
Thank you.

Mind Power. Focus gently on the area of your heart. Visualize golden light shining in your finances and business.

Sound Power. Chant silently or aloud:

Da Gan En (pronounced *dah gahn un*)
Da Gan En
Da Gan En
Da Gan En . . .

Chant for at least seven minutes. Use your heart to chant. The more you chant, the better.

Hao! Hao! Hao!
Thank you. Thank you. Thank you.

Gratitude is important in every aspect of life. As children, we have the greatest gratitude for the love and care our parents and grandparents gave us to raise us. In every level of school, we have the greatest gratitude for our teachers. At work, we have the greatest gratitude for all team members. For financial abundance and business success, we must have the greatest gratitude for Tao Source, Heaven, and all of our physical business team members.

A profound ancient spiritual wisdom is:

tian ren he yi

"Tian" means *the bigger universe, including Heaven, Mother Earth, spiritual fathers and mothers in all layers of Heaven, the Divine, and Tao Source.* "Ren" means *the smaller universe, which is a human being.* "He" means *join.* "Yi" means *one.* "Tian ren he yi" (pronounced *tyen wren huh ee*) means *the bigger universe and the smaller universe join as one.* Da Gan En, greatest gratitude, is a bridge to connect a human being with Heaven, so that they can join as one.

There is another sacred wisdom:

mo shi zai ren, cheng shi zai tian

"Mo" means *plan.* "Shi" means *things,* including business. "Zai" means *depends.* "Ren" means *human being* or *physical team,* which is also called *Mother Earth's team.* "Cheng" means *succeed.* "Tian" means *the bigger universe, including Heaven, Mother Earth, spiritual fathers and mothers in all layers of Heaven, the Divine, and Tao Source,* which are also called *Heaven's team.*

"Mo shi zai ren, cheng shi zai tian" (pronounced *maw shr dzye wren, chung shr dzye tyen*) means *planning depends on Mother Earth's team or the human team, success depends on Heaven's team.* Heaven is yang. Mother Earth is yin. Yin and yang are two. They are also one. *Tian ren he yi* is the yin and yang worlds joining together. When Heaven's team and Mother Earth's team join as one, great financial abundance and success can come much more easily.

Practice 9. Da Fu Wu (*Greatest Service*)

"Fu wu" means *service.* "Da Fu Wu" (pronounced *dah foo woo*) means *greatest service.*

The purpose of life is to serve. We have committed our lives to this purpose. To serve is to make others happier and healthier. I (Master Sha) cannot emphasize the earlier teaching enough: The root cause of success in finances and in every aspect of life is good karma from all lifetimes. Good karma is accumulated through great service for humanity, Mother Earth, animals, the environment, and much more. Great service includes love, care, compassion, sincerity, honesty, generosity, kindness, integrity, purity, grace, and much more.

I want to emphasize again and again why we are doing the ten Da Soul Over Matter practices. The ten Da qualities are the nature of Tao Source, which is the ultimate Creator. The ten Da qualities carry the jing qi shen of the Creator. The Creator's jing qi shen can remove jing qi shen blockages of our finances and business. The Creator's jing qi shen can nourish our finances and business. The Creator's power is Wu World power, which is unlimited. We inhabit the existence world, the You World. Everything in the existence world, including finances, is limited. We are extremely honored and blessed to practice with Tao Source to reap unlimited blessings and move toward unlimited abundance in every aspect of our lives. That is the power of the ten Da Soul Over Matter practices.

I also want to emphasize again and again: Why do we need financial flourishing? To receive financial flourishing is to be empowered to offer more service to humanity and to Mother Earth. Some very wealthy people have donated millions and billions of dollars to humanitarian services. These contributions are great. Money is energy. Remember the wisdom: Use money in the proper way, which is to help humanity.

Four sacred phrases share key wisdom of Da Fu Wu:

九大服務

Jiu Da Fu Wu

誓為公僕

Shi Wei Gong Pu

無私奉獻

Wu Si Feng Xian

上乘法門

Shang Cheng Fa Men

Jiu Da Fu Wu. "Jiu" means *nine* or *ninth*. "Da" means *greatest*. "Fu wu" means *service*. "Jiu da fu wu" (pronounced *geo dah foo woo*) means the *ninth of the ten Da Soul Over Matter practices is greatest service.*

Shi Wei Gong Pu. "Shi" means *vow*. "Wei" means *become*. "Gong pu" means *servant of humanity*. "Shi wei gong pu" (pronounced *shr way gōng poo*) means *vow to become a servant of humanity.*

In history, every major buddha, bodhisattva, holy saint, Taoist saint, and saints in other realms, including gurus, lamas, kahunas, shamans, healing angels, archangels, ascended masters, and more, have all made vows to serve humanity, Mother Earth, and all universes. They did this because they understood an important ancient sacred wisdom about vows and the spiritual journey. This wisdom can be summarized as follows:

> **Make a little vow and put it into action to serve humanity, Heaven, and Mother Earth, make a little progress.**

> **Make a bigger vow and put it into action to serve humanity, Heaven, and Mother Earth, make more progress.**

> **Make the biggest vow and put it into action to serve humanity, Heaven, and Mother Earth unconditionally, make unlimited progress.**

This spiritual wisdom also applies to financial flourishing. Grab the essence. Put this wisdom and practice into your finances and business.

Wu Si Feng Xian. "Wu" means *no*. "Si" means *selfish*. "Feng xian" means *offer, donate,* or *devote*. "Wu si feng xian" (pronounced *woo sz fung shyen*) means *selflessly offer, donate, and devote to help others and make them happier and healthier.*

Shang Cheng Fa Men. This phrase is connected with the previous phrase. It further explains selfless service. "Shang cheng" means *highest*. "Fa men" means *sacred gate*. "Shang cheng fa men" (pronounced *shahng chung fah mun*) means *selfless service is the highest sacred gate of Tao Source.*

These four sacred phrases can be summarized as follows:

Jiu Da Fu Wu. *The ninth of the ten Da Soul Over Matter practices is greatest service.*

Shi Wei Gong Pu. *Vow to be a selfless servant for humanity, Heaven, and Mother Earth.*

Wu Si Feng Xian. *Selflessly offer, donate, and devote to help make humanity, Heaven, and Mother Earth happier and healthier.*

Shang Cheng Fa Men. *The highest sacred gate of Tao Source is selfless service.*

In summary, Da Fu Wu can be summarized as follows for financial flourishing:

Offer little service, achieve little success and financial flourishing.
Offer more service, achieve more success and financial flourishing.
Offer unconditional or selfless service, achieve unlimited success and financial flourishing.

Let us do a Soul Over Matter practice of Da Fu Wu now by applying the Four Power Techniques. Do not skip the practices. They are the essence of soul over matter.

Body Power. Place one palm below your navel. Place the other palm over your heart.

Soul Power. Say *hello* to inner souls:

> *Dear soul mind body of myself,*
> *I love you, honor you, and appreciate you.*
> *The purpose of life is to serve.*
> *To serve is to make others happier and healthier.*
> *You have the power to join hearts and souls together to serve.*
> *Do a great job!*
> *Thank you.*

Say *hello* to outer souls:

Dear Source,
Dear Heaven and Mother Earth,
Dear all saints in Heaven and on Mother Earth,
Dear Da Fu Wu, greatest service,
I love you, honor you, and appreciate you.
My physical team members and I would like to serve more.
We would like to receive more blessings from Heaven and Mother
    Earth to serve more and serve better.
We are extremely grateful.
Thank you.

Mind Power. Focus gently on your heart area and visualize golden light shining in every team member associated with your finances and business.

Sound Power. Chant silently or aloud:

Da Fu Wu (pronounced *dah foo woo*)
Da Fu Wu
Da Fu Wu
Da Fu Wu . . .

Chant for at least seven minutes. Use your heart to chant. The more you chant, the better.

Hao! Hao! Hao!
Thank you. Thank you. Thank you.

Practice 10. Da Yuan Man (*Greatest Enlightenment*)

"Yuan man" means *enlightenment*. "Da Yuan Man" (pronounced *dah ywen mahn*) means *greatest enlightenment*.
    Four sacred phrases share key wisdom of Da Yuan Man:

十大圓滿
Shi Da Yuan Man

靈心腦身圓滿
Ling Xin Nao Shen Yuan Man

人地天道神仙梯
Ren Di Tian Tao Shen Xian Ti

服務修煉才可攀
Fu Wu Xiu Lian Cai Ke Pan

Shi Da Yuan Man. "Shi" means *ten* or *tenth*. "Da" means *greatest*. "Yuan man" means *enlightenment*. "Shi da yuan man" (pronounced *shr dah ywen mahn*) means *the tenth of the ten Da Soul Over Matter practices is greatest enlightenment.*

Every soul has its standing in Heaven's layers. To reach soul enlightenment is to uplift one's soul to the level of a saint. To reach heart enlightenment is to uplift one's heart to the level of a saint. To reach mind enlightenment is to uplift one's consciousness to the level of a saint. To reach body enlightenment is to develop a pure light body and live a long, long healthy life.

A human being has two lives: a physical life and a soul journey. The physical life is limited. The soul journey is eternal. Having flourishing finances and a successful business is only one aspect of one's physical journey. There are many other aspects, such as health, relationships, and intelligence, but ultimately the purpose of the physical journey is to serve the soul journey. This is the greatest wisdom that many spiritual seekers are searching for. Many people have not realized this wisdom and practice.

Why do we need financial flourishing? The more flourishing we have, the more we can serve humanity, Heaven, and Mother Earth. The more service we can give, the more our soul journey can advance. To uplift our soul, heart, and mind to the level of a saint is to be a better servant.

Think about holy saints such as Jesus and Mary, buddhas like Shi Jia Mo Ni Fo (the Chinese name of Siddhartha Gautama, the historical Buddha), A Mi Tuo Fo (Amitabha in Sanskrit), and Guan Yin (known as the Bodhisattva of Compassion), and many other saints in different traditions. Millions of people study, respect, and honor them because they are great servants for humanity, Heaven, and Mother Earth. In one sentence:

**The physical life is to serve the soul journey
in order to reach the greatest enlightenment.**

Ling Xin Nao Shen Yuan Man. "Ling" means *soul*. "Xin" means *heart*. "Nao" means *consciousness*. "Shen" means *body*. "Yuan man" means *enlightenment*. "Ling xin nao shen yuan man" (pronounced *ling sheen now shun ywen mahn*) means *soul heart mind body enlightenment*.

Complete enlightenment includes enlightenment of jing qi shen. Shen enlightenment includes soul enlightenment, heart enlightenment, and mind enlightenment. Jing (matter) and qi (energy) enlightenment combined are body enlightenment.

Ren Di Tian Tao Shen Xian Ti. "Ren" means *human being*. "Di" means *Mother Earth*. "Tian" means *Heaven*. Tao is Source, the Creator. "Shen xian" means *saint* or *heavenly being*. "Ti" means *stairs*. "Ren di tian Tao shen xian ti" (pronounced *wren dee tyen dow shun shyen tee*) means *there are stairs to go to Heaven and Tao Source*. These stairs represent the steps of the soul journey for human beings, Mother Earth, Heaven, and Tao Source. On the soul journey, every soul wishes to be uplifted more and more to climb Heaven's stairs and reach the greatest enlightenment of soul, heart, mind, and body.

To reach soul enlightenment, which is to have your soul reach the level of a saint, is a blessing beyond comprehension for one's soul journey. There are four major layers of saints:

- Human saint (lowest)
- Mother Earth saint
- Heaven saint
- Tao saint (highest)

To be uplifted to a human saint, then a Mother Earth saint, next a Heaven saint, and finally a Tao saint is to climb Heaven's stairs. The only way one can be uplifted to these layers is by offering unconditional service.

Fu Wu Xiu Lian Cai Ke Pan. "Fu wu" means *service*. "Xiu" means *purification of jing qi shen*. "Lian" means *practice*. "Cai" means *enable*. "Ke" means *can*. "Pan" means *climb*. "Fu wu xiu lian cai ke pan" (pronounced *foo woo sheo lyen tsye kuh pahn*) means *only through service can one climb the stairs of Ren Di Tian Tao* (human being, Mother Earth, Heaven, Tao).

The four sacred phrases for Da Yuan Man can be summarized as follows:

Shi Da Yuan Man. *The tenth of the ten Da Soul Over Matter practices is greatest enlightenment.*

Ling Xin Nao Shen Yuan Man. *Soul heart mind body enlightenment.*

Ren Di Tian Tao Shen Xian Ti. *Steps to reach different layers of saints are human being saint, Mother Earth saint, Heaven saint, and Tao Source saint.*

Fu Wu Xiu Lian Cai Ke Pan. *Only through service and purification of soul, heart, mind, and body can one climb Heaven's stairs to reach the saint levels of human being, Mother Earth, Heaven, and Tao Source.*

Da Yuan Man, greatest enlightenment, includes financial flourishing, but it goes far beyond. Da Yuan Man is to fulfill one's physical life and one's spiritual journey. Every aspect of being and every aspect of life will then flourish. This is the highest possible achievement of a human being.

Let us do the tenth and final Da Soul Over Matter practice now. Use the Four Power Techniques:

Body Power. Place one palm below your navel. Place the other palm over your heart.

Soul Power. Say *hello* to inner souls:

Dear soul mind body of myself,
I love you, honor you, and appreciate you.

You have the power to serve our financial flourishing.
You have the power to fulfill your spiritual journeys.
You have the power to serve unconditionally.
Do a great job!
Thank you.

Say *hello* to outer souls:

Dear Source,
Dear Heaven and Mother Earth,
Dear all saints in Heaven and on Mother Earth,
Dear Da Yuan Man, greatest enlightenment,
I love you, honor you, and appreciate you.
Please bless my physical team members and me for our financial
  abundance.
Please bless our enlightenment journeys.
We are extremely grateful.
Thank you.

Mind Power. Gently focus your mind on the heart area and visualize golden light shining in your heart, finances, and business.

Sound Power. Chant silently or aloud:

Da Yuan Man (pronounced *dah ywen mahn*)
Da Yuan Man
Da Yuan Man
Da Yuan Man . . .

Chant for at least seven minutes. Use your heart to chant. The more you chant, the better.

Hao! Hao! Hao!
Thank you. Thank you. Thank you.

The Soul Over Matter practices of the ten Da qualities are simple, practical, and easy to do. At this moment, you may not fully understand or appreciate their power and significance. Do not ignore them. Do not underestimate them. Practice them. Practice them more. Practice them a lot, with great sincerity, honor, respect, gratitude, and more. You will understand them more. You will appreciate them more. You will benefit more and more. I wish you to receive benefits of greatest financial abundance, business success, and flourishing in every aspect of your life.

PART THREE

Create Unlimited Abundance

9

Action Steps for Your Finances and Business

A S YOU CLEAR the soul blockages on the energetic and spiritual levels, including negative karma, you can also use the newly opened opportunities to apply the mind to achieve practical results in matter (the physical level). The next step is to shift your mind blockages. What limiting thoughts and beliefs are you holding that prevent you from reaching your dreams?

Shake Well: A Vaccine for the Mediocrity Epidemic

One of my favorite energy-boosting foods is a green drink—a blended concoction packed with healthy ingredients. The other day my wife brought one home for me. I was busy working, so I set it aside to enjoy later.

When I looked up after an hour or so, the drink had changed. The clear glass bottle, about eight inches tall, had been filled with a thick green juice. During the time the drink was sitting on my desk, the contents had settled, and now the top half of the drink had become crystal clear—almost as if the bottle were only half-full. In contrast, the bottom half had become even darker than before and was now a deep, rich shade of green.

The longer I stared at the bottle, the more I began to see there was more to it than just settled juice. The good stuff, the stuff that I paid the money for, the stuff that contained all the vitamins and essential minerals, the stuff I *wanted*—was all at the bottom. The relatively common and easy-to-find stuff—the tap water, basically—was at the top.

As I stared closer, I read the label:

Shake Well

Had I unthinkingly taken a drink of the juice without shaking it, I would have gotten nothing more than expensive tap water. Sure, it would have quenched my thirst and kept me hydrated, but it wouldn't have done anything extra for my health.

Unshaken, a good part of the juice was just another sip of the same old thing.

A Life Well Shaken

The stuff at the surface of life is not so different from the top of that unshaken green drink. It's easy to get at it. It's relatively flavorless. It's cheap. There's plenty of it, anyone can have it, and it takes no risk.

The stuff at the top is the same old job that pays the bills, but doesn't really give you *joy*. It's the same easy investment strategy that everyone uses, but that never seems to deliver *wealth*. It's the mindless shopping and endless screen staring.

That easy but flavorless stuff at the top?

It's mediocrity. It's average. It's safe.

It's the *status quo*.

When asked, though, most of us claim *we don't want the status quo*. We want a different income. Different things. A different body. A different job. A different relationship. And yet we defend the status quo like it's the last sip of water on the planet.

It's crazy when you think of it: to spend so much mental and emotional energy defending something we don't love or want. We're unhappy with our lives, and yet *we scrape and struggle to make sure we get to keep them just as they are*.

Why? Because we'll take the pain we know over the pain we don't know. The unknown is terrifying. As a result, we don't act on the little voice that tells us something is wrong. That tells us to go left instead of right—just *once*. To take a chance.

We don't listen to that voice. We don't move forward based on the wisdom of our heart or the inner knowing of our soul. Instead, we sit in our top-half life and protect the status quo.

And when that happens and we find ourselves defending the top half of the bottle, that's when we're dying a slow death. That's when we're living that quiet life of desperation.

The solution is to *shake well*. To step left, not right. To take a chance. To finally listen to that little voice so that we can take a sip of life that includes some of the richness from deep beneath the surface.

After all, the alternative is frightening. Like the juice, we settle. It takes time and it happens almost imperceptibly. But as we settle for mediocrity, our life settles, too. The good stuff gets deeper and farther away. It gets harder to see, harder to reach.

And finally, it decays and vanishes.

Shake well. It won't always be easy. It takes courage to move from the status quo—from the pain you know—toward an uncertain future. But this movement away from the status quo is the essential journey of our adult lives.

It's what we're here for—to dive deep and find the good stuff.

Financial Action Step 1

- Review your business and your finances. Where are you settling for less than the highest potential?
- Look at and question the things and systems "that have always been done that way."
- List options and steps to change what you have identified in your review and questioning.
- Make contingency plans for the changes you are planning in case the anticipated results do not materialize.

Don't Wreck the Car: Focus on What's Really Important

Oftentimes in business and life we are caught up in what is urgent, worrisome, or not working instead of focusing on how we can actually fundamentally change to create a different outcome.

Imagine a cold, rainy night. You're driving home from a party. It's late and you're tired. Visibility isn't great but you've driven this route many times. It's no problem.

As you come over a hill in the road, however, you receive a shock: There's a car broken down in your lane. You hit the brakes. Hard. With the wet pavement, it's clear you simply can't stop in time. The tires lock up and you begin to skid perilously on the wet pavement, sliding toward the looming wreck ahead.

What happens next depends entirely on *where you direct your attention.* If you continue to stare ahead at the stalled car that you're about to hit, you're almost certain to do what many do—you'll stand even harder on the brake, and you'll skid. And skid. And skid. And finally crash into the back end of the stalled car.

The same is true of money. When we focus our energy on financial problems on the road ahead, we have a tendency to skid right into them.

You can look constantly at your bills, your debt, or the paycheck that seems disappointingly small, but you're only staring at the stalled wreck of your financial life. You've got both feet on the brake, skidding in slow motion into another painful financial accident. The more you stare helplessly at the credit card bill or the mortgage payment you can't afford, the more time goes by, the closer the due date looms, and the more nothing changes.

As with the stalled car, however, there is another option. If you look elsewhere—if you direct your energy *away* from the thing you're about to hit—you might find that you can simply swerve to one side or the other and pass the stalled car safely.

When you narrow your focus to only the obstacles and not the opportunities, there's nowhere else to go but where you're already headed. As with traffic accidents, you have to be willing to look away from the obstacle. You need to have the presence of mind—the mindfulness—to direct your energy away from the negative, toward where or what it is that you want.

In other words, *you need to look where you want to go.*

To be fair, it's easy to be preoccupied by what you don't want. To worry about being unemployed or going bankrupt or becoming ill. And that's normal—those things do happen in life. But our preoccupation with them is a destructive habit.

Financial Action Step 2

The universe doesn't deliver based on what you want or don't want. It delivers based on *where you put your attention.* When you shift your attention elsewhere—away from the danger and toward what it is you want—you get different results.

Look at your current business and financial situation. Are you avoiding loss instead of thinking of how you can increase your reach and opportunity? If yes:

- List the main strategies you use in planning.
- Review them for defensive vs. strategic planning.
- Make a new list of opportunities that arise when you think strategically.
- Modify your decision-making and planning process in the light of this new perspective.

Avoid the Wreck: Shifting Your Thinking Habits

"I don't want to lose my job" or "I don't want to make another bad investment" are reasonable and common worries. But what if we shift the way we think about them? What if we look away from the looming financial wreck?

Consider these two examples.

Scenario 1: The economy is shifting and you find yourself preoccupied with job security.

What you habitually think might be:

I don't want to lose my job.

Imagine how this thinking might affect your work. Would you stop taking initiative at your job? Perhaps stop taking risks, just in case? Just put your head down and hope?

The more you focus on losing your job, *the less valuable you become at work*. And when layoffs occur, who's quickly rising to the top of the list? *You*.

What if instead you said:

What can I do to make myself invaluable to my company?

Focused on that idea, you might invest in learning new skills or take more initiative in your work. And the result? You're the last, not the first, to be let go. And if you are let go, you have a whole new skill set to start job hunting with.

Scenario 2: You made a bad investment in a business deal or lost money in the stock market.

What you habitually think might be:

I don't want to make another bad investment.

Focused on that idea, you might put all your money in a nice safe and secure savings account. Or under your mattress. And what happens? You earn less than inflation, meaning you're skidding even more quickly toward a financial crisis. You give up any possibility for compound interest, one of the most powerful financial tools in existence.

What if instead you said:

*How can I get better at analyzing investment opportunities
to make the best possible decision?*

Focused on that idea, you might begin to study stock market investment strategies. You might arrange to meet someone with a history of good business investments in order to learn more. And who knows—that meeting might turn into a lead on a great investment!

You can "rewrite" any financial worry this way. You can change your thinking in a way that casts your attention forward—beyond the status quo. Beyond what it is you don't want. Beyond the looming wreck and toward the safe passage to the road of opportunity ahead.

The above are real-life examples of our minds restricting our potential success and happiness. We can likewise use our minds to expand the possibilities and manifest more of the abundance we want. In business and life, exclusively focusing on the current situation is limiting.

Financial Action Step 3

Continue to elevate your thoughts and strategies to what will enable you to plan and devote your resources to create what you truly want: the goals and results that are in line with the flourishing business and life you seek.

- Analyze, find, and list the opportunities in the apparent risks you see in your financial situation.
- Develop a plan to take advantage of the challenges.
- Look around for help and support in achieving your goals—from your colleagues, friends, community, vendors, public services, etc.

The Gretzky Principle: Looking and Planning Ahead to Where You Want to Be

Nicknamed "The Great One," Wayne Gretzky is widely considered one of the greatest ice hockey players in history. What's most interesting about Gretzky, though, is that he had none of the hallmark attributes of a great ice hockey player. He wasn't particularly tall, heavy, strong, or fast—in fact, as far as hockey players go, he was unimpressive in all those areas.

What Gretzky *did* have, however, was an almost preternatural ability to *anticipate*. He had a knack for knowing where the puck would be and how to dodge checks from larger players. He seemed to always be able to put the puck in the right place at the right time, and the results were astounding. In his twenty-year career with the National Hockey League

(NHL), he scored more points than any player ever and still holds sixty NHL records.

Gretzky described it this way: "A good hockey player," he said, "plays where the puck is. A great hockey player plays where the puck is going to be."

This philosophy appears in many sports—football quarterbacks, for example, "lead the receiver," throwing the ball to where the receiver *isn't*, so that the ball and receiver meet at the right place and the right time. Cliff divers leap from the rocks when there's no water below so that the waves will have come back in by the time they reach the bottom.

This ability to anticipate isn't valuable just in athletics, but *everywhere*. You can learn, like a great quarterback of life, to "lead your thoughts."

If your current financial situation is one of struggle or scarcity, there's nothing to be gained by, in hockey parlance, passing the puck to that spot. You can't send your thoughts to where things *are*. You have to send them to where they would be if you were in a position to score. You need to pass the puck to a place of unlimited abundance. To a point in the mental future where your financial life is *as you wish it to be*. Where money is no longer a worry. Where great opportunities come your way. Where money shows up at your doorstep. In your mailbox. In your bank account.

The hardest part of this, of course, is to see that result and *to live as if it is so*, despite the current appearance that you're stuck. In hockey, to shoot the puck to a place where there is currently no player is danger-ous. For that period of time before the receiver arrives, the puck is free and alone and could be intercepted by the other team—a disastrous result.

It is, fundamentally, an exercise in faith. When a quarterback throws a ball to a space where there is no one there to catch it, he's operating on faith that his preparation and training are true. That his teammate, the receiver, will arrive as planned and catch the ball.

That moment when the quarterback releases the ball is a moment of faith. For cliff divers, the stakes—and faith—are even higher. Diving from a great height into the ocean, cliff divers must jump when the rocks are exposed.

For your personal finances, the stakes can also feel extremely high. To cast your thoughts to a point and to take action without guarantees is a challenge for many. It's an exercise in faith. But the inability to take that leap also keeps you stuck.

Without that faith, you live a life plagued with doubt. When you live with doubt, you live with fear. With worry. With scarcity.

As Gretzky also said, "You miss one hundred percent of the shots you don't take."

It's as true for money as it is for hockey.

Courting Energy: Expect, Plan, and Execute for Success

Imagine you've met someone. Your first date was phenomenal. And the second one? Even more so! You realize that you haven't just met some-one. You've found *someone*—a special person you think might just be *the one*.

Take a moment to consider what begins to happen in your life.

First, consider the shift in how you think. This new person is sud-denly at the top of your mind. You think about them first thing when you wake up. They're the last thing on your mind when you fall asleep. Throughout the day, you wonder what they're doing. You miss them. You anticipate when you might see them again, and you imagine in detail what you'll do, how you'll dress, and what you'll say. You think more about the other person than you do about yourself. You begin to look ahead more. And you find yourself becoming more positive.

Next, consider the shift in your actions. All this thinking is leading somewhere. First, you might call this new love interest and arrange a next date. You'll likely put energy into the work of courting. You try to be considerate or romantic or generous or funny. You might write them notes or call. You might surprise them with thoughtful gifts. You give of your time, spending more of it on that person instead of on your work, your friends, or your hobbies. When you're with them, you're more *present*. You listen more. You give more of yourself.

Now consider the results. Your thinking has clearly led to new actions. And what have those actions created?

You find yourself with a partner. You're happier. You've found the companionship that was missing. You have someone to share your life experiences with. You found *the one*.

What happened here is truly amazing when you consider it. Your change in thinking led to a change in action. And those actions led to a change in results. In effect, your thinking *transformed your life*.

When you were courting your romantic interest, you were doing more than wooing someone. *You were courting energy.* You were taking the intangible—your desire for love and companionship—and converting it into something *real*.

Right Thinking: Creating a Mental Equivalent

The changes in thinking that kick-started the romantic shift above are an example of what author Emmet Fox called creating a "mental equivalent."

When you become interested in someone, you begin to create a picture in your mind of a future that includes him or her. You imagine in detail spending time together. Taking trips. Enjoying romantic dinners or long walks on a moonlit beach. You create a detailed mental image of your life with that person.

This thinking isn't the same as the real thing—not yet, anyway. It's just a mental equivalent of the real thing. But it's the *right* type of thinking because it leads to different actions, which in turn lead to the real thing.

This "right thinking" is the first step in creating a different future. The right thinking leads to the right actions, which lead to the right results. It's a simple formula, and it applies to anything from love to careers, from money to health.

right thinking → right actions → right results

The trouble is that all too often, we want the *results* first. We want love without putting any thought or action into a relationship. We want financial abundance without putting any thought or action into our finances, career, or business.

Of course, it never works when we approach it that way because *the right thinking is a prerequisite.* It's a necessary first step to lasting success. It's why the Bible says, "For whosoever hath, to him shall be given, and he shall have more abundance." Those who *have* have already done the pre-work.

Over time, you begin to habitualize right thinking. It becomes not something that you consciously do, but simply something you *do*, like driving your car or brushing your teeth. That right thinking is the prerequisite. And when you've done that work, you continue to do more of it without thinking. You gain momentum.

Better still, the energy of your thoughts can be transformed into more than just romantic outcomes. You can create *anything* using the same principles, including financial abundance.

You can, in effect, court money with the same shift in thinking that you might use to woo a partner. What if you gave more energy to your financial life in the same way you would give more to a love interest? What if you thought more about the future, in vivid detail? What if you imagined how you might earn more, save more, or be more fulfilled at work? What if you painted a detailed mental picture of abundance?

What actions do you think you might take?

And what results might you receive?

Financial Action Step 4

Plan for what is to come. The saying from the film *Field of Dreams*, "If you build it, they will come," has some basis in fact. When you take a calculated risk and stretch your imagination and efforts, and direct your resources to where your elevated expectations are, you have a much higher probability of achieving greater success than if you were timid in your goals and plans.

- Establish your upgraded goals.
- Share them with your colleagues and loved ones to solidify and deepen your commitment to your goals.
- List and implement the new steps you need to take to achieve your increased financial abundance.

Ice Cream, the Universe, and You

Our family has spent many a summer in Martha's Vineyard. After years of observation, I've come to the conclusion that the economy of this small island off the coast of Cape Cod, Massachusetts, runs on three things: real estate, T-shirts, and ice cream. As the father of four kids, I've made more than my fair share of contributions to the ice cream economy, and along the way, I've learned an important lesson about money and the universe.

Imagine for a moment that, like me, you're an abundance-minded person. You believe that the universe is a kind and loving place and that we're an extension of that. You believe we all come from the same source of infinite intelligence. You know the world runs better on love and that feeling abundant is a state of being that makes everything better.

Now imagine you're standing outside a quaint ice cream shop. Beside you is a perfect, adorable little girl who at this moment is looking up at you with big eyes, saying, "Pwease? Can we have ice cweam? *Pwease?*"

What do you do?

If you're like me, you end up in the ice cream store. What other choice is there? You believe in love and limitless abundance, right? So inside you go, and you order up a cone, and you sit back and bask in the wonder that is the universe.

But as surely as this abundant universe contains ice cream, it also contains—at least in our store—a heavy wooden door with an automatic closer. And in a statistical anomaly that I still don't quite understand, that heavy wooden door somehow manages to swing closed against the arm of any child under the age of five who's holding an ice cream cone.

And so there you are, watching in slow motion as that adorable little girl, staring raptly at her cone, heads out the door—the door that at this moment in the perfect universe is closing rapidly on her arm. You reach out to stop it, thinking, *nooooooooo.*

An instant later there's a fresh, barely licked ice cream cone in a puddle on the floor and a young child staring up at you with the deepest, most profound look of disappointment that you can imagine. Those same big eyes are now filling with tears. Everyone in the store has turned to look at this unspeakable tragedy.

At this point, what do you do? You believe in abundance. *Limitless abundance.* You think the world runs best on loving kindness. And those *eyes.*

Do you buy her another cone?

Sure you do.

So you head back inside. But this time, something different happens. The child, who's made a miraculous recovery from the brink of emotional collapse, looks up and sees a poster with a picture of an ice cream cone with *three scoops.* Each one is a different, amazing color. It's *The Triple Scooper.*

She stops. Stares. Then turns to you with those big eyes.

"Daddy?" You know what's coming. It's hurtling toward you as surely as that door hurtled toward the first cone. "Daddy? Can we get that one? Can we get the twiple scoopa? *Pwease, Daddy?*"

What do you do? You believe in abundance. Limitless abundance. Infinite, limitless abundance. And *those eyes.*

Do you buy her The Triple Scooper?

If you're like almost everyone in the audiences I've told this story to around the world, you practically cry out, "Yes!"

Unfortunately, the answer is *NO!*

Yes, the universe is infinitely abundant. There's enough ice cream for everyone. But here's the rub: The universe is also kind, loving, and generous; it doesn't intentionally set anyone up for failure.

Why, then, would you be any different? Why would you give three scoops to a child who can't handle *one?*

The lesson here for your desire to attract more material abundance is that right now, you're holding what amounts to a single scoop of financial ice cream, and it's a *mess.* You've got debt. Bills you haven't paid. You have no budget. You're spending more than you earn. Your single scoop cone is melting and dripping down your arm. It's slopped on the floor and smeared down the front of the shirt you bought with a maxed-out credit card. And worse still, the automatic door of financial reality is about to slam on your arm.

Yet despite all this, in financial terms you're asking for The Triple Scooper. You want more, yet *you haven't shown that you can handle what you have.*

The universe isn't going to give you more money to drip down your arm when that money is only going to hurt you. It's not going to bless you with more money if that money will only allow you to dig a deeper hole. It won't frustrate you or give you something you're not equipped to keep.

We always get just as much as we can handle. If you want more, *the first step is to handle what you already have.* Learn to manage your current money, *however small it may be.* Take ownership for your current financial ice cream cone. Learn to manage even the tiniest scoop, and the universe will reward you with more.

Financial Action Step 5

- Take inventory of your current financial situation.
- Prioritize your resources to the items that will most support the vision you have developed in action steps one through four.
- Work out a plan to reduce and eliminate the items that are not in line with your goals.
- Review the allocation regularly, at least once a month. Adjust your plans and allocation accordingly.

Learning to Receive

In the book *The Richest Man in Babylon*, author George S. Clason lays out the timeless principles for building wealth in a series of simple parables.

In the book, two friends in ancient Babylon, frustrated with their lot in life, visit their old friend Arkad, who is the wealthiest man in Babylon. Arkad reveals that he too was once poor, but learned a critical lesson from a wealthy man:

"I found the road to wealth," the wealthy man told Arkad, "when I decided that *a part of all I earned was mine to keep.* And so will you."

This principle, which becomes the first of "seven cures for a lean purse," isn't original—the "pay yourself first" rule has been repeated, restated, and reworked an untold number of times over the years. The idea of taking some portion of your income and setting it aside for investment to grow your wealth is fundamental to almost every financial plan on the planet.

It's easy to see the wisdom in this, and the simple math of setting aside ten percent of your income so it can compound over time isn't difficult.

What many people fail to realize, however, is the deeper, spiritual lesson contained in this simple idea.

When you are able to put aside ten percent, you're demonstrating that you can manage what you have. Like a child wanting a triple-scoop ice cream cone, you're not going to receive it until you can safely deal with the single scoop in your hand. Paying yourself first is the single most tangible piece of evidence that *you're ready for more.*

Of course, many people respond to this idea with shock: *I won't be able to pay my bills if I set aside ten percent.* And in that thinking, they perpetuate the problem by saying what amounts to "There isn't enough."

Of course, there *is* enough. Necessity is the mother of invention, and it's remarkable how resourceful we become when we have to. Most people find that a ten percent change in their income isn't that noticeable.

We use the same faulty thinking when it comes to charity and tithing. "Once I have enough money," we say, "I'll give to charity." But somehow there's never enough, and we never give.

But the lesson goes deeper still. Deciding that a portion of what you earn is yours to keep is also about *learning to become a receiver.* It's about learning to accept gifts from the universe.

Money is energy. It's a renewable resource that's circling us, flowing through us and around us. But before you can tap into that flow, you have to be willing to receive it. To do that, you need to do more than just *say* that you're ready. You need to demonstrate it.

Each time you choose to pay your bills before you pay yourself, *you are denying your right to receive.* When you decide "I'll pay myself what is left over," what's left over is usually nothing. What's left is you, broke and continuing to remain separated from the energy of money that's flowing around you.

Deciding that a portion of what you earn is yours to keep is more than a simple math lesson and more richly nuanced than the decision to open a second bank account. When you take *any* amount, no matter how small, and pay it to yourself first, you are taking the first steps to becoming a receiver and the first steps to tapping into the energy of money.

Financial Action Step 6

- Put your "non-negotiables" into your budget—a minimum percentage for investment/savings and for giving back/charity.
- Apply the same principles to your company budget—a percentage for investment and research and a percentage for community/charity outreach.
- Acknowledge that you, your company, and the charity you choose deserve to be considered priorities in your business and life.

Alignment, Money, and Flow

Back when I was still a Peaks student and was just beginning the journey that would eventually lead me to the role of CEO, I attended what we called Enlightened Warrior Camp, a multiday training event designed to help people access their will to succeed and to overcome any obstacle.

It was the first night of the five-day program, and as part of the evening's exercises we were divided up into four different "tribes." One of our first jobs as a tribe was to create a tribe cheer. A number of people in my group were leading the activity when a woman approached, squared off in front of me, and cocked her head.

"Why," she asked, "aren't you leading?"

I was taken aback but laughed it off.

She persisted. "You're a leader," she said. "Why aren't you leading? Why are you playing small?"

We'd only barely started the program and I didn't even know the woman's name, but that moment was like an assault on my heart. It was as if she'd seen straight through me.

As she stood there, awaiting an answer, a voice inside me asked, *Why ARE you playing so small in your life? What are you afraid of?*

It was a pivotal moment. I felt something shift inside me, and from that incident on, I led in that camp. It not only transformed my experience of that week, but also kick-started my path to becoming a trainer with the company and, eventually, the CEO.

What I would eventually realize was that, in that moment during the training program, I had made a shift toward *alignment*. For perhaps the first time, my thoughts, my words, my actions, and my *heart* had been pointed in the same direction, toward the same goal, with the same intention.

When I was an attorney, my thoughts, words, and actions were anything but aligned with my heart. For years, my heart had been telling me *you are a teacher*. And for years, I'd ignored it, pretending not to notice the signs of unhappiness until they finally landed me in the emergency room.

This misalignment has profound consequences. When you align your life, you align it at a deep, energetic level that has physical effects on the world around you.

For a long time, people believed that the world was made up of *stuff*. Matter. Bits of particles, jammed together. Subatomic particles came together to make atoms. Atoms connected to make molecules. Molecules connected to make earth, and water, and air, and wood, and living things.

But the smarter we got, and the closer we looked, the more we realized that all that *stuff* was really just *energy*. Pure energy, vibrating and moving about, coalescing and taking shape in the form of the physical things we could see and touch. Pure energy *flowing*.

Your house is just energy. Your car, your clothes, your food? More energy. And yes, money, like everything else, is also energy. A one hundred dollar bill is made of the same fundamental energy *you* are. At an energetic level, you and money are essentially the *same thing*. All that differs is the vibrational frequency of that energy.

When you align your actions, words, and thoughts with your heart and soul, you allow energy to flow. Thoughts and decisions become clearer. Actions become easier. Everything that once felt difficult and forced becomes fluid and effortless. It's as if you've been swimming up a river, struggling and gasping for air, and suddenly you realize you can turn and go with the flow.

Financial Action Step 7

- Review your personal mission and goals and match them against your allocation of time, effort, and resources.
- Review your company mission and goals, and check for the alignment between them and how you direct and manage your employees, budgets, plans, time, outside resources, and vendors.
- Realign your personal time, effort, and resources to what is really important to you. Make a list of the steps you are going to take to reposition them to reflect your true priorities.
- Work with your team to reallocate your various resources to address the discrepancies between your company mission and goals and your current use of human, financial, and network resources.

Mental Broccoli

In 1935, the spiritual leader Emmet Fox published a short pamphlet called *The Seven Day Mental Diet: How to Change Your Life in a Week.*

Fox's diet had nothing to do with carbs or red meat or sugar. Instead, his idea was as simple as it was powerful: to go a full week without holding or expressing a negative thought.

Like its physical counterparts, *The Seven Day Mental Diet* falls squarely in the category of things that are simple but not *easy.* To follow the diet, you must avoid sustaining fear-based thoughts like condemnation, judgment, anger, resentment, self-doubt, and scarcity. Instead, your new mental diet should consist of powerful, positive thoughts like gratitude, kindness, optimism, love, and abundance.

It's no easy task. In fact, if anything, The Seven Day Mental Diet is even *harder* to stick to than a food diet. At first. What's critical to note, however, is that the goal isn't to never *have* negative thoughts. We all have those, and to attempt to *never* think them is an exercise in futility. What Fox's mental diet asks you to do is to not *sustain* those thoughts. Simply notice them, and change your thinking.

This is a critical distinction; the thoughts that we dwell on or consistently entertain are the ones that guide our lives. They drive our actions, which in turn create our results. If you consistently entertain negative thoughts, over time you'll see the negative effects in your life.

At first, this isn't an easy idea to stomach. It can be hard to see the connection between negative thoughts and the results in life, but they are there. To help, I often tell students to think of the positive thoughts as the "broccoli" of thinking.

We all know broccoli is good for us. It's packed with vitamins and minerals that support our biochemistry in a multitude of ways. It's an accepted truth that broccoli is nutritious.

If you don't *like* broccoli, it's still good for you. If you don't believe it contains vitamins, that's fine—but they're still there. Whether you believe it or not, broccoli is good for your health.

The same applies to the thoughts of the mental diet. You don't have to believe that positive, abundant thinking is good for you. Like broccoli, it just *is*. And, like broccoli, you should try it . . . you might discover you like it after all.

Financial Action Step 8

- Do you have areas or topics that you and your team avoid thinking about or planning for?
- What are the sacred cows in your company?
- What do you take for granted as *givens* in your market? And in the world? Things may not be as fixed or as certain as they seem.
- Review and discuss the assumptions and take a fresh look at both what may have been regarded as guaranteed and what was thought of as unlikely or impossible.
- Research and make plans to address potential unseen risks and opportunities.

You've come to the end of this chapter on the action steps of how to achieve greater financial abundance. Some of the insights from the stories and action steps may be familiar to you, and others may be completely new; contemplate and integrate them now into your daily life, and reenergize the knowledge and practices that you already know and do. When you combine these with the Soul Over Matter practices, you will have a solid foundation upon which to build and expand your finances and business. Congratulations and many blessings to your success.

Conclusion

IF YOU ARE flourishing in your business and finances, it is because you have served well in this life and your past lives. Service is the key to financial abundance.

If you are lacking in your finances and business, this book provides the wisdom, as well as practical and powerful tools, for your positive transformation. The three sacred ancient words, jing qi shen, and the Soul Over Matter practices of the ten Da qualities could transform your finances and business beyond your expectations. To practice the ten Da qualities is to accumulate virtue because you are bringing the ten Da qualities to humanity and Mother Earth. You are serving humanity and Mother Earth. The virtue that you gain from your service will bring you financial abundance.

Soul over matter is the ultimate path to unlimited abundance. We hope that you benefit from the wisdom, tools, stories, and valuable insights in this book on how to achieve financial abundance and more. The highest accomplishment we can attain in life is to live a life of service, helping others live happier and healthier lives. The side effects of assisting others are that we are blessed with much more in the process. We clear our negative karma and create good karma, both of which enhance our lives in numerous ways.

We can illustrate how this process works with a memorable experience of one of the authors of this book. When Marilyn Tam was president of Reebok Apparel and Retail Group, she wanted to improve the working conditions and wages of the apparel factory workers Reebok's contractors used around the world. She witnessed the dimly lit, poorly ventilated, noisy, and crowded factories, where primarily young girls and women were packed in rows working long hours with very limited breaks for hygiene or food. The workers seemed more like indentured servants than free agents employed in a business.

Marilyn wanted to change that. Her own management team at Reebok was very concerned and resisted her proposal to demand positive changes in the industry standards for apparel factories and their workers. Her CFO, Operations VP, Productions VP, Merchandise VP, and Sales VP all argued with her that their vendors owned the factories and that Reebok had no right to tell them how to operate their businesses. They argued that making changes would raise prices, delay production, create bad relations with their suppliers, and overall make Reebok uncompetitive with the rest of the apparel market. Ultimately, they said such demands would make Reebok's apparel business suffer, create a bad reputation for the footwear division, make their contractors and retailers unhappy, and cause many to lose their jobs.

Yet Marilyn felt that there was a better way to produce apparel that did not cause many people all over the world to work punishing hours for low pay and no benefits, to the detriment of their health and long-term prospects. She believed in soul over matter. She believed that serving others and making them happier and healthier was going to be good for everyone in the long run.

Being a businessperson in control of a large purchasing budget, she had strong negotiation power with the factories. And being the president, she chose to exercise her prerogative to make the final decision on this contentious issue. However, as she is also a strategic person, she created practical steps in implementing the change. As Master Sha explained in this book, there is a Heaven's team and an Earth team. The Earth team needs to take care of the logistics and contingencies in any major decision.

Marilyn approached Reebok's most important factory group and asked them to choose one of their best factories and one of their lower-performing ones for an experiment. She asked the factory owners to institute regular breaks; improve ventilation so that the workers could breathe air free of the dust, lint, and fumes created by the fabrics, accessories, and chemicals; increase lighting so that the workers could see better; pay living wages; hire only workers over eighteen years old; and reduce working hours so that workers had time to rest. As part of the agreement, Reebok would accept the production of the goods even if they were late or substandard. The experiment was a risk for both sides.

When the first production run was finished, everyone was in for a surprise. Both the top factory and the lower-producing one improved on all aspects of production, attendance, and more. The goods were completed ahead of schedule, the defect rate was significantly lower than usual, the quality of the workmanship was high, and the absentee-ism rate due to illnesses was reduced. Because of the early completion, the goods could be shipped by boat instead of by air, which resulted in further savings. When the goods arrived on the retail sales floor, they sold well and the retailers were pleased, as was Reebok's management team. It was a success on all levels. Most of all, it showed the power of listening to one's soul. When we are aligned with soul over matter and consider service before profit while taking into account the practical/ earthly aspects, we can flourish beyond expectations.

With this initial success, Reebok and the factory group developed a system and set of working standards that were eventually enacted in all Reebok contractors' apparel production factories and countries. From there, the system and standards gradually spread through networking and collaboration to the entire apparel industry. Like many things in life, changes continue as apparel production expands to more locations and countries. The lessons have to be learned and relearned by the new-comers. This same concept of soul over matter applies for everyone and everything, no matter where you live or work. The good news is that the greater the awareness and consciousness, the faster the higher consciousness can spread. Practice the ten Da qualities and study the meaning of the three sacred ancient words that Master Sha shared. This will increase your good karma, clear blockages to your success, and grow your financial abundance.

Resistance and fear are often by-products of growth and change. Choose to step away from fear and lack—disapproval from others, threat of monetary loss, and even the risk of losing one's job. Trust that as we follow our soul's guidance, eventually we will prevail. Marilyn had a lot to lose on paper and very little to gain, but her soul knew that she could make a bigger, positive difference if she pushed for the change. Take the risk, shake off complacency, and dare to reach higher. Do what you were born to do and be who you were born to be: a being who brings more light to the world.

**Serving humanity unconditionally is the true secret
to create financial abundance.**

Appendix
Soul Over Matter in Action

H ERE ARE TWO examples of Soul Over Matter business success in the real world.

The Body Shop

During the writing of this book, the authors had the rare pleasure of meeting with Gordon Roddick, cofounder with his late wife, Anita, of The Body Shop beauty and health care products. It became apparent during the interview that the success of The Body Shop is an excellent illustration of the fundamental principles of soul over matter. The insights we gained from our conversation about the success of The Body Shop may encourage you to center your own business activities in soul over matter consciousness and action.

Anita and Gordon founded The Body Shop in 1976. They had minimal money at the time and started with a single store. They did not have a grand vision of creating massive wealth or reaching tens of millions of consumers. Anita had been a history teacher and Gordon an agricultural expert. They were barely staying afloat financially, but they had a vision and a basic sense of goodness about how their products should be created, marketed, and sold. Anita in particular was concerned that other companies were emphasizing packaging, advertising, and marketing and not focused on creating excellent products with superior ingredients.

Anita and Gordon decided from the very beginning that they would put the product first, give their customers the best products possible, and worry less about marketing. They also decided that everyone they worked with would be treated fairly. They went out of their way to ensure that the people and companies producing their products would be compensated fairly, even if that increased their own costs. The only people they hired in their company were ones who shared their humanitarian and social values, and they encouraged their staff to devote time to community service.

Anita and Gordon wanted everyone associated with The Body Shop to understand that the primary purpose of the stores was to provide service, not just to customers but to the entire community. Profit was necessary to ensure the health of the company, but maximizing profits was never a core company concern. Giving back and helping to create a better world was the "soul" value of the company. This soul value was seen in their treatment of their employees, suppliers, and customers and, in a deeper sense, in their commitment to their local and eventually global community.

In 2006 when The Body Shop was sold to L'Oreal, there were more than two thousand stores throughout the world. Today there are more than three thousand shops. Anita died much too young, but Gordon and their daughter Justine continue the spirit of The Body Shop's original core value of giving back in multiple ways. Their direct charitable gifts to humanitarian causes are in excess of $2 million annually.

One of their unique investments is the creation of an incubator for start-up companies and entrepreneurs dedicated to creating higher-consciousness companies whose products and services create a healthier, happier world. The spirit of Anita Roddick lives on through the good works of Gordon and Justine and the millions of people who have been inspired by The Body Shop, a company that believed in soul over matter from the beginning.

The Sacred Space

A less dramatic but equally representative soul over matter story is that of Jack and Rose Herschorn. Jack has always followed his heart, and his heart has taken him in many directions. Jack has been in the music industry as the founder of a record company, a music publisher, and a recording studio owner; a chiropractor; and the creator, together with his wife Rose, of Jack's Famous Bagels in Santa Barbara, California. Ten years ago, he and Rose founded a unique emporium in Summerland,

California, called The Sacred Space. The Sacred Space sells books, jewelry, spiritual artifacts, and beautiful objects that Jack and Rose source from exotic locations throughout the world. When you enter The Sacred Space, you are offered a cup of tea to enjoy in the meditation garden. There is no charge for the tea and no rules on how you use your quiet moments sipping tea, as long as you do not disturb others enjoying their tea in this sacred space. If you choose to purchase an item in the adjoining shop, your patronage is appreciated, but whether you purchase or not, you will be greeted with smiles and appreciation for your visit.

On the surface this seems a very strange way to run a business, but it works and is working better every year. The reason it works is that both Jack and Rose are in service to humanity and the planet. They do not ignore the business requirements necessary to ensure that they are profitable, but like The Body Shop, profit has never been their primary purpose. As Jack told us when we interviewed him, "I never seem to generate high profitability when I focus on the money. If I just focus on what I love, on allowing my customers—even if for just a few minutes—to enter a place of higher consciousness, I do best. I enjoy every aspect of The Sacred Space: from the sourcing trips to India, Bali, Thailand, and Nepal where Rose and I meet highly talented artisans, to hosting events for spiritual teachers here in Summerland. We meet the most interesting people on the planet coming through our front door, in our travels for items, and as teachers at The Sacred Space. It is a big win for us to do what we love and to be on a path of evolvement to be all we can be at the same time."

Postscript

Jack and Rose have not yet read this book, as we are just finishing it now, but because of their support in providing The Sacred Space Private Retreat in Summerland, California, where much of this book was written, we want to acknowledge that the soul of their business is perfectly aligned with the core principles of soul over matter abundance consciousness. Master Sha met Rose and Jack a little less than a year ago when he gave a lecture at The Sacred Space retail store and gardens. Master Sha was so moved by the goodness of Jack and Rose's hearts and souls that he blessed their enterprise with a financial blessing. They have reported an increase in sales of more than twenty percent month-over-month since receiving Master Sha's blessing. Jack expressed their appreciation and personal experience of interacting with Master Sha and the impact of his blessing in the following words:

I really don't know exactly what occurs, but something happens with Master Sha. In my mind I've thought his energy, in some way, removes my personal energetic blocks to the realization of my full potential.

Rare is the person who feels uninhibited to their own full potential or has an actualized true belief in their unlimitedness, and even rarer is the person who can transfer that to another.

I believe Master Sha does this.

Acknowledgments

Master Sha

I thank from the bottom of my heart the beloved saints and the Divine, Tao, and Source Committees who flowed parts of this book through me. I am so honored to be their servant and a servant of humanity and all souls.

I thank from the bottom of my heart all of my beloved spiritual fathers and mothers, including the late Dr. and Master Zhi Chen Guo, the founder of Body Space Medicine and Zhi Neng Medicine. Master Guo was one of the most powerful spiritual leaders, teachers, and healers in the world. He taught me the sacred wisdom, knowledge, and practical techniques of soul, mind, and body. I cannot honor and thank him enough.

I thank from the bottom of my heart Professor Li Qiu Yun, who chose me as the sole lineage holder of the unique long stroke calligraphy form called Yi Bi Zi, Oneness writing, which you see in the Tao Source Calligraphies in this book. I cannot honor and thank her enough.

I also thank my beloved sacred masters and teachers who wish to remain anonymous. They are extremely humble and powerful. They have taught me priceless secrets, wisdom, knowledge, and practical techniques, but they do not want any recognition. I cannot honor and thank them enough.

I thank from the bottom of my heart my physical fathers and mothers and all of my ancestors in all of my lifetimes. Their love, care, compassion, purity, generosity, kindness, integrity, confidence, and much more have influenced and touched my heart and soul forever. I cannot thank them enough.

I thank from the bottom of my heart my co-author Adam Markel for his wisdom and knowledge for this book. I thank my literary agent and his wife, William and Gayle Gladstone, for their love and great contribution for this book. I also thank Dr. Marilyn Tam for her great wisdom, knowledge, and contribution for this book. I cannot thank them enough.

I thank our publisher, BenBella Books and Glenn Yeffeth. His unconditional support has touched our hearts deeply. We cannot thank him enough.

I thank from the bottom of my heart all of my Worldwide Representatives and Divine Channels, who have typed my flows for this book, designed the cover, edited the book, and more. My Worldwide Representatives are servants of humanity and servants, vehicles, and channels of the Divine. They and all of my business team leaders and members have made incredible contributions to the Divine and Tao Source mission. I thank them all deeply. I cannot thank them enough.

Last, but not least, I thank from the bottom of my heart my dear family, including my beloved wife, daughters, son, mother, brother, sisters, and more. They have all loved and supported me unconditionally. I cannot thank them enough.

I am extremely honored to be a servant for you, humanity, and all souls.

Love you. Love you. Love you.

Thank you. Thank you. Thank you.

I love my heart and soul
I love all humanity
Join hearts and souls together
Love, peace and harmony
Love, peace and harmony

Adam Markel
I wish to acknowledge the Source of all that we are for inspiring the kinship and collaboration that resulted in *Soul Over Matter* being created. I want to personally, and from the deepest place in my heart and soul, thank Master and Dr. Sha, Bill Gladstone, Marilyn Tam, Master Cynthia,

Master Allan, Master Elaine, my beautiful and always supportive wife Randi, and our unique and amazing children Chelsea, Lindsay, Max, and Eden for being in my life and adding their love to the recipe that baked this wonderful book.

Blessings, Blessings, Blessings

Love, Love, Love

Adam

Index